Parsifal
and the Search for the Grail

Charles Kovacs

Parsifal

and the Search for the Grail

Waldorf Education Resources

Floris Books

First published privately in 1998
This revised edition published in 2002

British Library CIP Data available

ISBN 0-86315-379-8

Printed in Great Britain
by Mackays of Chatham

Contents

Foreword

British authors who have written of the great legends of King Arthur and the Knights of the Round Table have said little of the story of Parsifal. To Mallory it is Gawain who holds a central place, with Parsifal (Sir Percival) relatively unimportant; others have concentrated on the romantic tales of Lancelot and Guinevere.

And whilst acknowledging the British origin of these legends it is to the troubadours of France and Germany, notably Chrétien de Troyes and Wolfram von Eschenbach that we need to turn for a complete rendering of the wonderful story of Parsifal.

Rudolf Steiner recommended this story for pupils of Class 11 in the Waldorf education curriculum (age 16–17 years) as a way of introducing them to world literature and to one of the central problems of our time — the journey of the consciousness soul and the imperative to learn to ask the right questions. Like Parsifal they will all go through their own individual way of finding the Grail as a requirement of living in this century.

This publication has come about in response to requests from other interested teachers. It is taken from original notes written in 1965 as preparation for a Class 11 main lesson.

Charles Kovacs

The original text has been lightly revised by Peter Snow in 2002.

1

Minnesingers and Troubadors

I am going to tell you in these lessons a story called the story of Parsifal. It is a very old story — going back to the twelfth and thirteenth centuries — and that brings me to the first question we have to ask: why should anyone today bother about an ancient tale — a tale from the Middle Ages, a tale of knights and castles and swordfights? What can a story of medieval knights mean to us who live in the present age of computers and space travel?

Well, perhaps it is a good story — and a good story is always worth telling. After all, Shakespeare's plays were also not written yesterday — yet they have the power to move the hearts of people nowadays. Great works of poetry don't age — they are above fashions which come and go — they span the centuries, they are bridges between past and present. And the Parsifal story, as it was composed some eight hundred years ago, is one of these great works of poetry.

Yet — this isn't the reason why I want to tell this story to you. If it were only a matter of making you acquainted with some great of work of literature outside the English language, I might as well have chosen the German poet Goethe's tragedy *Faust* — a play about a man who sells his soul to the devil. Or, perhaps, the Italian poet Dante's *Divine Comedy* — which is not a comedy at all, but the description of a journey into the depths of hell and to the heights of heaven. As great creations of literature, they are just as important as the Parsifal story. But there is a different reason for taking Parsifal.

And to give you this reason for taking Parsifal, I want to tell you of two events which actually happened — they are not stories invented by a poet's mind.

The first event took place during the Second World War in

America. It was about 1943 or 1944, and by that time science fiction had become very popular. Quite a number of writers specialized in this field, and had their stories published in one or other of the science fiction periodicals. One of these writers sent in a story which was promptly published — a story about a new kind of weapon. But as soon as this magazine appeared in the bookstalls, the American FBI — the Federal Police — confiscated the whole issue and arrested the author. He was accused of a breach of state security — because the weapon he had described in his story was the atom bomb. And at that time the atom bomb was still a closely guarded military secret — the first experiments at Los Alamos were still under way, and not a whisper of it had yet reached the public. And now — there was this writer who had described the main principle of it, the fusion of uranium, in his science fiction story.

The poor man was in danger of a stiff prison sentence — but, fortunately for him, he could prove that he knew nothing at all about the Los Alamos experiments and that the story he had written was only the product of his own imagination. He had not betrayed any secrets, because he had never been told any. So he was released in the end, with a stern warning — and only years later, when the secret was a secret no longer, could he tell how he barely escaped from a trial for high treason.

And now we go back a bit further — 2,500 years ago — to Athens in ancient Greece. It is a public holiday, and the people of Athens are gathered in the great amphitheatre to watch the first performance of a new play by their favourite playwright, Aeschylus. The author himself takes part in the play — he is one of the actors. The play begins — there is deep silence in the audience. And now Aeschylus, the author, in his part, steps forward and speaks his lines. But he is suddenly interrupted by a wild outcry from somebody in the audience: "He betrays the holy Mysteries! Stop him! Kill him!" And in the same moment, men with drawn swords storm on to the stage. Aeschylus runs from the stage — he escapes from his pursuers and reaches the temple of Dionysos. Here he has at least a temporary sanctuary — because no fugitive can be taken from the temple.

And now Aeschylus asked for a proper trial before the judges of Athens. This was granted to him, and he stood trial for having betrayed the secrets of the Mysteries — a crime punishable by death. But, fortunately, Aeschylus could prove that he had never been initiated into the Mysteries, that he had never been told any of their secrets and so could not betray them. His play, and every word in it, was only the product of his own imagination. And so he was allowed to go free.

It is a strange parallel, isn't it? between these two events — a strange similarity — although they are separated by a long stretch of time — about 2,400 years.

Yet, at either end of this long stretch of time there is the same situation; there is a closely guarded secret, known only to a small circle of men — and there is one person who — out of his own resources, out of his own ingenuity — discovers the secret for himself.

There is this striking similarity — but there is also a very striking, a very significant difference.

The difference lies in the kind of secret which is closely, so jealously guarded.

What kind of secret was it, that the Mystery temples of ancient Greece kept, and which was only divulged to chosen men and women?

In the Mystery temples, the seekers for truth were shown a way to higher worlds — to the worlds of the spirit. The secrets of the Mystery temples were secrets of the spirit.

And what kind of secrets are those which led to the atom bomb? The physicists, the scientists who in the end produced this monster weapon were, at first, not at all searching for a weapon of destruction. Their research had quite a different purpose. For a long time, science believed that all matter, all physical matter, was composed of atoms. *Atom* is a Greek word which means: indivisible, something that could not be divided. But, after the discovery of radium, it became quite clear that matter could be further divided than atoms — that the atom could be divided into smaller particles — electrons, neutrons, protons, photons — and there are even, as we now know, particles of negative matter.

You see — the scientists worked on the secrets of matter.

The atom bomb was a by-product of the search for the secrets of matter.

So you have in the Mysteries of ancient Greece, secrets — but they were secrets of the spirit — and you have in modern times, in the experiments of Los Alamos, secrets of matter.

In the 2,400 years which lie between the two stories I have told you, humankind has gone from the secrets of the spirit to the secrets of matter. The science fiction writer got into trouble because he had "guessed" some of the secrets of matter — the Greek playwright got into trouble because he had guessed some of the secrets of the spirit.

There is this long stretch of time — 2,400 years — and at one end there are secrets of the spirit, and at the other end there are secrets of matter. And there is a third kind of secret in the middle between them. What kind of secret could it be?

I would like to leave this question as a question. We shall, perhaps, find an answer to this question as we go on with these lessons. But there is, at least, a name for these secrets, these third kind of secrets. There was a time when people were deeply concerned with this third kind of question or secret — and they called these secrets: *the secrets of the Holy Grail.*

And the story of Parsifal is the story of a man's search for the secrets of the Holy Grail.

And what is the time of the Parsifal story? The time of Parsifal lies roughly — very roughly — in the middle between the time of Aeschylus and the time of the atom bomb.

The Parsifal story stands, one could say, in the middle between two ages: one — the age that looked for the secrets of the spirit — was coming to an end; the other age — that was going to search for the secrets of matter — was just about to begin.

Now imagine some kind of superhuman intelligence looking down on earth at that time — a superhuman being that could look back into the past, and that could also foresee the future trend of human progress. And this being would ask itself: "Is it possible to save something of the old world for the new world? Is it possible to save the secrets of the spirit for the time that will only look for the secrets of matter.?"

And in answer to this question, this being would invent the story of Parsifal — a story in which the secrets of the spirit are brought together with a modern mind, the kind of mind we have today. *And Parsifal, the hero of this story, is really a modern man, the first modern man — a man who has a modern mind — although outwardly he follows the customs of his time.*

And, you see, this is the reason why we are doing the Parsifal story — because Parsifal is really a modern man, in spite of the medieval trappings. He stands on the threshold between two worlds.

I said "a superhuman intelligence might have thought up this story of Parsifal." I don't know if such a superhuman intelligence existed, but the fact is that in a period around the year 1200 not one but several poets produced Parsifal stories. There are great differences between the stories — no version is exactly like the other, but the main features are the same.

And, you know, in their time these stories were what we would call "bestsellers" — they were extremely popular. Bestsellers is, of course, a wrong word. There were no publishers to print the story, because printing had not yet been invented. Moreover, most of the people who wanted to know the story could not read — they had to listen to professional storytellers who moved from place to place, from castle to castle.

And the telling was not in prose — it was in verse. The stories were long poems which the storytellers recited — they even sang them, and used a harp as accompaniment. Some storytellers could only repeat what they had learned from others. But some could and did invent their own stories — they were called *troubadours* (from *trouver* = find).

The stories made up by the troubadours were all about knights and their deeds — King Arthur, Lancelot, Gawain. One of the first troubadour who introduced a knight called Parsifal was a Frenchman, Chrétien de Troyes. People were not so nationalistic in those times as they are today, and Chrétien de Troyes was quite content to have as his heroes British knights. King Arthur is, of course, a British king — and Parsifal, too, is British. He is called "Parsifal le Gallois" — Parsifal the Welshman.

The next troubadour who composed a Parsifal story was a German knight, Wolfram von Eschenbach.

Wolfram is a remarkable person. As a knight, he was trained and brought up to be a fighter, to know how to handle spear and sword. And so, when he describes a fight, he speaks with the authority of an expert. But the education of a knight did not include such useless arts as reading or writing. Wolfram actually mentions in one passage of the poem that he never learned a single letter of the alphabet.★ Perhaps he was being ironic.

But this is a long poem — in modern print it covers some four hundred pages. It is so long that I would not even attempt to tell you the full story. You will have to be satisfied with a very abbreviated version — otherwise the story plus the necessary explanations and comments would take far more time than we have.

I am afraid you would also be bewildered by the many other heroes and other stories which are interwoven in the story of Parsifal — it is a cavalcade of his whole time which Wolfram presents, and you would hardly be able to cope with all the names of knights and their ladies and how their lives meet and cross the path of the main hero, Parsifal.

This medieval German is, of course, very different from modern German. For instance, Wolfram's words "I can't read a single letter" are in the original *"ine kan decheinen buochstap,"* which even the best of you in German would not recognize.

There is still one more thing to be said about these long poems made up by troubadours like Wolfram and Chrétien de Troyes.

They wrote or dictated these works for the entertainment of

★ Wolfram's insistence that he was illiterate has long been a crux for scholars. It is unsafe to assume that he was indeed illiterate. He wrote other works beside *Parsifal*, notably *Titurel* and several love lyrics. While it may not extend credulity too far to suppose that he dictated *Parsifal* and *Titurel* to an amanuensis, the writing of love lyrics suggests that Wolfram was not incapable of taking up a pen himself. Otherwise, we have to imagine a monk so magnanimous as to make himself available to Wolfram for a great deal of his time. This seems unlikely to me, though I am not an expert in the practices of medieval monasteries. It is generally supposed that Wolfram was not rich, and that he died in comparatively young., The usual interpretation of *Parsifal* scholars is that Wolfram was exercising his gift of irony at the expense of other medieval poets who wore their learning less lightly than did Wolfram himself. *PS.*

lords and ladies — and in this way they are the forerunners of the modern novelists. Then stories were the novels, the popular fiction of the twelfth and thirteenth century.

But the troubadours aimed much higher than mere entertainment. They made these stories an instrument to convey their religious convictions, their highest ideals, their philosophy of life. Yet they managed at the same time to introduce humour, to go from tragic moments to comic situations — to touch the deepest problems of human life, and at the same time to relish the description of a good fight.

It is this skilful blending which makes such a thing as Wolfram's *Parsifal* a true work of art, a great poem.

And, as it is with every good novel, you should, after going through Parsifal, feel that you have learned something, not about a person who exists only in the pages of a book, but about yourself. That is what, in the end, all literature is about.

2

The Boyhood of Parsifal

I have given you the general background of the Parsifal story — where it stands in history — and I have also told you of the troubadours, the poets who composed, each in his own way, different versions of the story. And, as I said, I shall follow mainly the tale as told by Wolfram von Eschenbach, but draw also from Chrétien de Troyes and others, for there are beautiful scenes in each of them. So — here begins the story.

Spring had come to the countryside, it had come to the fields where the first leaves came from the dark earth, it had come to the vast forest of Saltane where oak and ash trees put out their first green buds.

It was a great forest, and even a man on horseback would have taken days to cross it. But only a few paths led through the close ranks of the trees, and only rarely did a wanderer pass on these roads.

But well away from the roads, deep in the heart of the forest of Saltane, there was a clearing and a few simple huts and a little patch of ground, tilled and worked over by human hands. Strange that people should choose to live so far away, so cut off from their fellow beings.

But spring has come — it had come to the forest and to the clearing, and as the forest birds twittered and sang to greet the morning a youngster, the son of a widow, came from one of the huts in the clearing. He carried short hunting spears, and over his shoulder a bow and a quiver of arrows.

The youngster was proud of his skill with the hunting spears — no roebuck had ever escaped his aim. But the bow was a new thing: he had fashioned it himself only the day before, and he was eager to try it out.

Deeper he went into the forest, and started to practise with bow and arrow. At first his targets were trees, but he soon got tired of aiming at motionless tree trunks. Then he saw a bird perching on a branch. The youngster quickly took aim and let fly, and saw the bird fall. But — strange — the lucky shot gave him no pleasure ... it made him feel sad, it made him feel guilty, it made him feel ashamed. Why was this? Puzzled, the youngster turned homewards to the clearing in the forest. To whom should he turn but to his mother for an explanation of this strange sense of guilt?

Beside him and his mother, there lived only a few men and women in the clearing, simple ignorant people who served them and worked the land. They would not be able to answer his question. And beside his mother and the few servants, he had never in his young life seen another human being. The forest and the clearing were all he knew of the world. And so the youngster came to his mother, and asked her: "Why did the killing of a bird make me feel sad?"

And the mother said: "It is because you have, without need, taken the life of a creature, a life that God gave."

"God?" said the youngster. "Who is God?" And the mother replied (and here I use the version in verse):

> Son, He is brighter than the day
> And, once, to help man on his way
> He lived as man on earth indeed.
> To Him you turn in every need.
> But dark is he who by his art
> Makes men from God's true ways depart.
> From him keep free your soul and heart.

It was, perhaps, a simple instruction. But for this youngster who lived such a simple life, cut off from the world, it was all he needed. All the knowledge he had — and it was very little — was of this simple kind, and his mother told him nothing that could rouse his curiosity about the great world outside the forest. He knew nothing about the way people lived outside his own world — the forest.

And so, having satisfied his question, the youngster went out into the forest again, happy to walk on the soft moss and to listen to the song of the birds.

But suddenly he heard other sounds in the distance — hoofbeats, and the clatter of steel against steel. He had still fresh in his mind what his mother had just told him, and he said to himself: "Perhaps this is the Evil One, the black master of evil — I will have my spears ready, and deal with him in a way he shall never forget."

And so, eager for this encounter, he hastened in the direction of the noise. But what he saw as he came nearer made him stop in his tracks.

He saw five figures mounted on horses. Each of them was clad from head to foot in steel, and as the sunlight fell on the metal the rays were reflected and made each figure shine, so that it dazzled the eyes. They also carried great shields painted in brilliant colours, and long spears and swords.

The youngster had never seen anything like it. But had not his mother told him that God was as bright as the day? Surely, these dazzling beings must be God.

And so, as the riders passed where he stood, he fell to his knees and lifted his arms and cried out: "O God, help me — O God, give me your blessing!"

As he had fallen to his knees right in front of the first rider, the whole company had to stop. The first rider said to his companions, "The young fool here must be out of his mind with fear. He might be able to help us in our search, but I have to get some sense into him first."

And then he said to the kneeling figure in the road, "Don't be afraid of me, my good lad."

"Afraid?" said the youngster, "Why should I be afraid of you? I am not afraid of God. Are you not God?"

"No," said the rider. "I can assure you I am not God. But I want to ask you a question. Have you seen two men and a lady passing this way?"

The youngster paid no attention to the question. He stood up, but continued to stare at the riders. And then he said, "You are not God — well, then, I can only say that you are more beautiful than God. Oh, I wish I were like you! And if you are not God, what are you?"

"Upon my word," said the rider, "we have run into the silliest creature of this forest. My good lad, I am a knight."

"A knight," said the youngster. "I have never heard this word before, but I can see it must be the most wonderful thing in the world to be a knight. And what is this?" he asked, pointing to the shield.

"Look," said the knight, "we are in a hurry. Have you seen two men and a lady?"

But the youngster had no ears for the question. "Tell me," he cried, "tell me what this is, and what it is for?"

"Heaven help me!" said the knight with a sigh. "This thing is called a shield, and I use it to protect myself against an enemy's spear or arrow."

"And what is all this shiny stuff on arms and breast?"

"It is called armour," said the knight, "And it also protects me against sword-strokes and the points of spears."

"How wonderful!" cried the youngster, "but I am glad that the roebucks in the forest don't have such armour. If they had, my mother and I would rarely have any meat to eat. But, good knight, tell me — were you born that way, with a shiny armour on you?"

"No," answered the knight with great patience, "no-one is born with armour on his body. I was given this armour when I was made a knight."

That was good news for the youngster — he cried, "Oh, one can be made a knight! Tell me quickly who makes knights, so that I can go to him and also become a knight!"

"Our master, King Arthur," answered the knight, "can raise men to the noble ranks of knighthood. But now, my lad, make way for us. I see that you cannot help us, but we are in haste, and must get on."

And as the company continued their journey, the first knight said, "I wish I had the good looks of that boy — there is no better-looking man in King Arthur's court. But what a pity that with those fine looks and strong body there is the mind of a nitwit. May heaven protect the poor lad!"

But the youngster stood for a long time, looking after the knights, until the glitter of armour could be seen no longer, and the hoofbeats could no longer be heard. The little world in which he had lived so long was shattered for him, and his mind was in turmoil. There was now only one thought, one wish in his soul — to find King Arthur and to become a knight with shield and sword and armour.

The forest and the clearing that had been his home, the faithful servants — even his mother — were no longer things that mattered to him: they were like shadows compared with the burning wish, "I want to be a knight." And with this decision in his mind, he hurried homewards.

His mother was waiting for him with great anxiety. It was long past the time when he should have been back. At long last she saw him coming, and though she felt relieved to see him safe and sound, she received him with reproaches. Did he not know how worried she would be? Why had he kept her waiting so long? What had kept him in the forest? But her son was a changed person.

He took no notice of her agitation, he offered no apologies, but burst out, "Mother, I have seen the most beautiful thing in the world!"

"Have you?" said the mother, astonished. "What was it?"

"You remember," said the son, "you told me once that the most beautiful beings in the world are the angels. But you are mistaken; I have seen today something more beautiful than angels ever could be."

"Good Lord in Heaven!" cried his mother. "You can't be in your right mind to talk like this. What has come over you?"

But the son answered, "No, mother — I really saw these wonderful beings, and I even know what they are called. They are called 'knights'."

At the sound of the word *knights,* the mother's face became deathly pale, and then she fainted. The son stood there in dumb amazement. What had he said which could upset his mother so much? With the help of some servants, the lady was laid on her bed, and after a time she recovered consciousness. She sent the servants away, and then said to the youngster, "My dear son, for many years past, my life has only had one purpose: to prevent you from knowing that there is such a thing as knighthood, or knights. You should not see knights, you should not hear of knightly deeds. You should remain in ignorance of anything that has to do with knights. And you come and utter this hateful word to me, and destroy all I have worked for all these years."

"But why?" cried the son. "Why did you want to keep from me this knowledge? Why should I not know of knights?"

"You shall know why," said the mother. "There never was a better knight than your father. No-one was better loved by his friends, no-one was more feared by his enemies. Of noble blood was he, and so am I, the daughter of a family of high lords and kings. And great were our possessions; great lands were ours, and hundreds of knights were at our service. But by evil and by treachery your father lost his possessions, and he died fighting his enemies. You were the only one left to me, a little child, and in my grief over all I had lost, I promised myself you should not die as your father had died — you should not be tempted to risk your life for the glories and honours of knighthood.

"That is why I came, with a few faithful servants, to this wilderness, far away from the world of knights and their lust for battle. I gave up all the comforts, all the honours that were still my due, so that I could bring you up in this solitude, safe from the evil ways of the world — safe from the lure of knighthood. And now that I have told you, my dear son, I hope you will see that there is nothing but death and sorrow in the pursuit of knighthood, and you will forget the knights you have seen."

But her son only shook his head, and said, "All you told me cannot change my mind, mother. I want to become a knight, I want to go to King Arthur, and life would not be worth living if this were denied to me. O mother, you must help me — give me a horse and let me go to King Arthur!"

For many days, the lady argued and pleaded with the boy, but he, who had never before disobeyed her, was now changed. He paid no notice to her grief, he paid no notice to her pleading and only repeated stubbornly, "I want to become a knight."

So the poor woman thought, "Perhaps if I dress him up to look foolish and give him an old mare that can hardly walk any longer, people will laugh at him and mock him, and he will soon turn back and return to me." And so she made him a shirt from sackcloth, and clothes made up of different patches sewn together, and a hood with flaps on either side — it was the usual garb of fools who amused princes with their antics. And she gave him the oldest, most miserable-looking horse she could find as his mount. But the boy, who knew nothing of the ways of the world, was as happy as a lark. Here were clothes to ride out in, here was a horse to carry him, here was a light, slender hunting spear to protect him — what more could he want?

In his mind, the whole wide world lay open before him, ready to be conquered: King Arthur and his court were only waiting to receive him, and to accept him as one of them — a knight.

He did not notice how, in the last days before his departure, his mother's face became ever more haggard, he did not notice that she hardly ate anything, he did not hear her sobbing through sleepless nights. His own nights were illumined by beautiful dreams in which he saw himself as a knight of King Arthur, and when he was awake he thought of nothing else.

And so came the day of his departure. He said his goodbyes quickly, for he was impatient to be on his way — he spurred his old horse into a canter, and so he rode away, without once looking back.

But his mother stood and watched as long as she could see him, and when he was out of sight, the grief was more than her weakened body and a heart tried by a lifetime of sorrow could bear. A merciful, sudden death delivered her from the loneliness and worry and pain that would have been her fate.

But the son, not knowing that he had seen his mother for the last time, not knowing that his departure had been a death blow to her, rode on, singing gaily, through the dark forest and into the world.

Outsiders and Caspar Hauser

This rather strange upbringing which left a young man, at the age of about seventeen, completely ignorant of any useful knowledge. That he could neither read nor write would not have mattered a great deal in those days — but he also knew nothing of the customs, of the way of life outside the forest.

There was a civilization, the civilization of the early Middle Ages, and this young man was a complete stranger to it — which means he was a stranger to his own time. He was in the same position as a modern child brought up on a desert island — and suddenly at the age of seventeen brought into a modern city.

Of course, the young man — like the modern child I mentioned — would after a time, after many mistakes and blunders, pick up what he needed to know: young people can adapt themselves to all and any conditions, and this young man would not be any exception. He was bound to have some surprises in store for him — but, eventually, he was also bound to adapt himself to the new world outside the forest. But the first seventeen years of his life, spent in the forest, cut off from the civilization of his time, were also bound to leave their mark on him.

The first seventeen or eighteen years of life are the formative years, as they are called — they form one's whole attitude to life. Later on one may acquire far more knowledge, gain experience, make a career — but the fundamental attitude to life one has acquired by then, and this will remain throughout life.

Let us take a concrete example from history. There was in the eighteenth century a young heir to the throne of France, Louis. Prince Louis was, as a child, a clever and charming little fellow. The courtiers who surrounded him, his royal parents, they all doted on him. They petted him, they praised him, they fussed about him. No wish was ever denied to him — in short, he was thoroughly spoilt. At the age of seventeen, Prince Louis became king — he became King Louis XV of France. He easily picked up the other forms of kingship — the air of superiority, the gracious smile. But he was quite unable to shoulder the responsibilities of a ruler of a great nation. He could not face the work, he could not face the worry of making decisions. And so he soon left the whole task of government to an ambitious woman — his mistress, Madame de Pompadour. The result was a series of disasters for France which, thirty years later under his son, led to the French Revolution.

You see, the first seventeen years had left their mark; it was these years which made Louis XV the kind of person he remained to the end of his life.

Now, the young man in our story had not been spoilt in this way, but his upbringing in the solitude of the forest had made him a stranger to the whole civilization of his times — he was a stranger to his own time. Outwardly he would soon adapt himself — and even enjoy doing so — but in his heart he would remain a stranger to it or, to use another word, he would remain an "outsider."

Outsiders are people who live in a certain time, who take part in all that goes on in that time, often very successfully, yet they do not really fit — they are like beings from another world.

A typical example of such an outsider is Leonardo da Vinci. Leonardo was greatly respected in his own time — princes competed for the favour of having him work for them. Nor did Leonardo ever lack friends — he was never without companions who sincerely loved him, supported him, and stood by him in times of need. Yet the one thing that mattered most to him — his search for knowledge, his scientific pursuits — were centuries ahead of his time; there was no-one with whom he could share this burning interest, and he had to keep it all in the pages of his notebooks. And so Leonardo, who was so popular as a person, so successful as an artist, was all his life a lonely man, an outsider.

It is this inner loneliness which made Leonardo an outsider in his own time; and the young man in our story was, by his strange upbringing, doomed to the same kind of inner loneliness. But, you know, this inner loneliness is also the very thing which brings people like Leonardo or this young man so near to us. We can feel with them, with can sympathize with them, we understand them — and there is a reason why we can understand them so well: because nowadays each one of us is living in just this kind of inner loneliness.

No doubt everyone of you has good friends, close friends. Yet — you know it — there is something in you which remains alone and separate, something that remains alone even when you are in the midst of a crowd of friends.

This inner loneliness is, in a way, the foremost problem of modern man, and has become the central theme of a great part of modern literature in every country.

Some writers treat this inner loneliness of modern man as something sad and tragic. A French writer used the word "exile" for it: "I feel like a man living in exile — in a foreign land."

Other writers — Samuel Beckett for instance, the man who wrote *Waiting for Godot* — makes a wild, furious joke of this loneliness.

Another French writer, Sartre, takes this loneliness to its utmost extremes — to the point where this loneliness becomes so precious to you that you hate all other persons — and he put this feeling into the words, "Hell is other people." It is, for Sartre, a kind of hell to have to live together with others.

And there are the writers who seek to escape from this loneliness by the use of drugs. By the use of cocaine and heroin they withdraw into a heaven and a hell of their own making. There are other drugs to get away from one's ordinary self and its loneliness — mescalin, marijuana or Ecstasy.

And it is not surprising that it is young people who go in for this kind of drowning the loneliness in drugs — because it is the young people who feel that loneliness more sharply, more intensely, than some older people.

But in books written one hundred, two hundred, three hundred years ago — or earlier — you will not find anything about this loneliness, which is the best indication that it was not a general problem. There were the lonely ones, the outsiders, at all times, but they were the exception, not the rule. There were a few people who lived in our kind of loneliness, people like Leonardo, or like the young man in our story.

In our time this loneliness is as natural as the air we breathe — we all have to bear it. In past ages it was not so — it needed special circumstances to produce it. And it is nothing less than a feat of genius that the troubadours, these poets who lived eight hundred years ago, wrote that story of the mother who withdraws with her son to the solitude of the forest, and so creates just the kind of special situation which would make the child an outsider — a lonely modern soul that had to live in the world of eight hundred years ago.

It would be an unnatural upbringing at any time — to withhold from a child the knowledge, the schooling, the education which existed at that period. And you might think it would be a terrible hardship if you were in a similar position and you had to catch up — now, at your age — with all the things other people of your age had learned already. You might think it would be a hard and terrible thing if you had to start from scratch now.

But, as a matter of fact, something like that did happen to a real person. A real person was once, like the youngster in our story, brought up in complete ignorance and then, without preparation, thrown out into the world. But, in this true and historical case, the motive for keeping the child cut off from the world was not a mother's mistaken love, but sinister intrigues.

The story of that unfortunate real person who had a similar upbringing to our young man — this true story — is one of the great unsolved riddles of history. Many books have been written about it, but none of them gives a satisfactory answer.

The facts — the historical facts — of this mystery are these:

The place was the city of Nuremberg in Bavaria, in southern Germany. The time was 1812. One fine day in May of that year, a citizen of Nuremberg going for a walk outside the city gates saw a young man in peasant dress who seemed to be drunk, for he could hardly walk. The citizen, being a kind person, offered help to the young man. He discovered that the lad's feet were bleeding, and that he could only speak a few words which made no sense. He certainly was not drunk.

The man took the strange youngster into town and, eventually, the poor creature landed up with the Nuremberg police. The police, too, could not make any sense of the few words which the lad repeated again and again. But when given a piece of paper, he wrote on it in stiff, clumsy capital letters the words CASPAR HAUSER. Obviously he had been taught to draw these letters without knowing their meaning, but the police assumed that this was his name. As it was impossible to find out where he came from, the police lodged him in an unused prison, in a tower.

At first it was thought he was a village idiot who had somehow got away from his home; he was about sixteen or seventeen years old, he could not walk properly — he walked like a child taking its first steps — he could not speak, apart from a few words like "horse" and "rider," and as he could not speak he also could not think.

The first three things we learn at the age of one to one-and-a-half are walking, then speaking, then through speaking, thinking. This boy of seventeen had no real command of any.

However, his eyes had none of the dullness of a mentally retarded person — there was intelligence in the way he looked on his interrogators, and so the police were greatly puzzled by this Caspar Hauser. Moreover, he picked up new words with amazing speed, and once he knew the meaning of a word he never forgot it, and used it correctly. Other strange things about Caspar Hauser were that he would not touch any food except dry bread and water — and that he could see in darkness as well as in daylight.

The mayor of Nuremberg ordered an investigation, and a host of lawyers, doctors, government officials descended on Caspar Hauser in his tower. As a result of their investigation, the mayor announced that this young man possessed excellent intelligence, that he was of a goodness and purity rarely to be encountered, but that somehow his whole upbringing had been criminally neglected. And, in conclusion, the mayor decided it was the duty of the city of Nuremberg to look after the poor boy.

It created a kind of sensation in Nuremberg. People came in droves to visit Caspar Hauser, as if he were a strange beast, and they plagued him with questions, which the bewildered boy could not answer. He showed, however, an angelic patience and friendliness to all who invaded his tower.

However, one of these visitors was a school teacher who took a warm personal interest in the youngster. He spent many hours teaching him new words, and was amazed at the speed with which his pupil learned. And, at his request, Caspar Hauser was given into his care.

Teaching had, of course, to start from scratch — he even had to learn to walk. Yet, within three weeks, Caspar could converse fairly fluently, he had mastered arithmetic and could play simple tunes on a harpsichord. And he could read and write — all within three weeks!

But there were other things to wonder about. One afternoon, the teacher found his pupil sitting in the garden, absorbed in a book. Swallows circled around his head, pigeons picked crumbs at his feet, a cat purred in his arms, and butterflies had settled on his shoulders. On other occasions, too, he showed a strange power over animals. A vicious dog, kept chained by a neighbour, broke his chains and came snarling and snapping through the hedge — but lay down peacefully at Caspar's feet and licked his hands. Caspar could not think evil of any person — and he called all the people he saw "beautiful." He could not understand what a lie was — and he could not tell one himself. For a long time, he spoke of himself only as "Caspar," and it was a great discovery when he understood the pronoun "I," and learned to use it.

His power of memory was quite extraordinary. People read to him long lists of names, or figures — hundreds of them — and he could repeat them immediately in the right sequence and without a single mistake. Moreover, he was astonished that not everybody could do it. The young Caspar Hauser was an amazing person.

But as he was now able to speak, he could also throw some light on his unknown past, and what he told, and retold, and wrote about it, constitutes the greatest riddle in the mystery of Caspar Hauser.

The earliest thing he could remember was a dark room — a

little room containing a bed and a chair, and nothing else. He was chained to the bed, and could go no further than the chair. He was alone in the darkness, and never saw any human being at all. When he woke from his sleep, he found a slice of bread and a jug of water on the chair; he never saw the person who put the food there whilst he slept. On occasions, the water tasted different — he slept longer than usual, and when he woke up he found himself washed, his hair cut and a new bucket for his bodily needs. He had no idea of time, he did not even know that he was lonely — he vegetated, and knew nothing, thought nothing, heard nothing and saw nothing.

This state must have gone on for years, for it was only a short time before his release that, whilst he was awake, the door of his prison opened and somebody came in. That somebody spoke a few words, again and again, until Caspar repeated them. These were the first words of human language he had heard, and learned without knowing what they meant. This somebody also made him copy the signs on a piece of paper which meant "Caspar Hauser." It may have taken a couple of days, until this somebody was satisfied. Then he took Caspar Hauser out of that dark cell and, as he was unable to walk more than a few yards, the somebody put Caspar on his back and carried him, with frequent rests, a few miles. For several days, Caspar was moved in this way, and then the somebody left him standing just outside Nuremberg, and walked off.

This revelation roused a storm. Newspapers demanded an explanation, they demanded an investigation to find out who had committed this inhuman cruelty. And some people openly accused a noble and ruling family in Germany of having disposed of some awkward relation — a possible heir to the throne — in this ghastly manner.

A German High Court judge undertook to solve the mystery, and Caspar Hauser was transferred to his care. And then the school teacher who had started the whole thing died suddenly and unexpectedly ... and then the High Court judge died just as unexpectedly — and then Caspar Hauser was stabbed to death by an unknown assassin who was never found. And the mystery of Caspar Hauser has never been solved.

The story is told by a German writer, Jakob Wassermann in *The Enigma of Caspar Hauser,* which has also been made into a film.

The reason why I told you the story of Caspar Hauser is that here we have a real, not a fictional, account of a child brought up in ignorance and cut off from the world. Yet, this child let loose on the world at the age of seventeen was, two years later, so far on that he could study Latin, and translate Julius Caesar.

If you remember the fantastic speed with which Caspar Hauser learned, if you remember his equally fantastic memory, you will realize that being kept back had not reduced his intelligence — quite the contrary, it had enhanced and strengthened his mental capacities.

If the authorities which lay down the laws of education paid attention to this terrible "experiment" that was made two hundred years ago, they would not insist that children of six — or in some schools, five — should learn to read and write. I am quite convinced that you all here would just walk through your exams if your schooling had begun, let's say, at ten, or twelve, and not at six. But, things being what they are, we shall have to go on as we do now.

The fact is that the human mind grows stronger if it is not burdened too early with knowledge, as the case of Caspar Hauser shows. And — to return to our story — the strange upbringing of our young man, which made him an outsider, a lonely soul, in his time, this upbringing which kept him back, also gave him a keener mind, it gave him greater abilities than if he had been brought up in the ordinary way. Our young hero was not at such a disadvantage as it may seem.

Parsifal's Early Adventures

You will have noticed that I spoke of the hero of our story all the time as "the young man" or "the youngster," without using his name. But in doing this I am only following the troubadour, Chrétien de Troyes, who also calls his hero for the first chapters of the book only "the young man" — and there is a good reason for this: because this young man does not know his name. And this comes out in the next events of the story, which I shall now continue.

The young man, decked out in the fool's garb his mother had given him, and mounted on his old mare, rode happily through the forest, and then out into a world of ploughed fields and villages that he had never seen before.

From time to time, he met other people on the road — a peasant driving a mule, a merchant in a horse-drawn cart. They looked with some surprise at this fellow in fool's dress, and smiled at him. But he took this only as a sign of friendliness, and greeted them with the words, "I bid you a good journey — as my mother has told me," which made them smile even more, but none of them thought of mocking one who was obviously simple-minded.

And then the road he followed led him through a mountain pass, and riding down a slope he heard a woman's voice — but it was a sound of wailing and crying and sobbing. What could this be? Driven by pity as much as by curiosity, the young man turned his horse in the direction of the voice, and coming round a bend of the path he saw a young woman sitting on a rock — in her lap was a man's body ... it could only be a dead body, as the stiffness of the limbs indicated.

The young man approached the crying woman, and said, "Lady, my mother told me to offer my services to any woman in distress. So let me help you in your misfortune." The woman lifted her head, but she only looked at him in silence.

Unabashed, the young man continued, "Tell me, who was it who killed this knight you mourn? Tell me who it is and, I promise you, the murderer shall not escape from my spears — I shall make him pay with his life for the grief he has caused you."

It must have seemed strange to the woman that this lad, without shield or armour, and carrying no better weapon than hunting spears, offered to go and slay an enemy who was bound to be superior in arms and in experience. But she recognized that it was not youthful boasting that had moved the young man, but the true spirit of chivalry. And she answered, "My young friend, I honour your good intention, but there is no call for you, a stranger, to revenge the death of this knight, who was betrothed to me — who was my bridegroom. He for whom I grieve was not murdered, but slain in open battle, face to face with the enemy. But you have a noble heart to offer yourself to the service of a stranger — tell me, what is your name?"

"'Good son, dear son' — that was the name by which my mother called me," answered the young man.

At these words, the woman looked long and silently at him — and when she spoke again, there was a different tone in her voice. "Is this only name you know?" she asked.

"It is, indeed — and what better name could I be called by my mother than 'good son, dear son'?" said the young man, a little impatiently.

And again the woman looked at him in silence before she said, "Well do I know her who called her child by these names — for she is my aunt, Queen Herzeloyde, who went to hide herself and her little son in the forest many a year ago. Queen Herzeloyde was your mother's name, and I am your cousin, Sigune. But you, too, have a name, dear cousin, given to you when you were born — and may God make it a name to be honoured. Your name is 'Parsifal'."

"So, I am Parsifal," said the young man in wonder. "But, cousin Sigune, you called my mother Queen Herzeloyde. Is she a queen, then?"

"Yes, Parsifal," said the woman, "because your father, the noble Gamuret, was king of the land of Norgals. And when he and your elder brothers lost their lives in combat, and when your mother Herzeloyde took refuge in the forest, this knight who now lies dead in my arms, my bridegroom, took upon himself the task of holding and defending it until the true heir — you, Parsifal — could come and wear the crown. It was your land he defended, and it was whilst fighting against a foreign invader that he whom I loved lost his life."

"Then it is my duty to avenge him and to regain my kingdom!" cried Parsifal. "Sigune, you must tell me which of the roads that meet here shall lead me to the enemy, and I shall not rest until justice is done, and my kingdom restored!"

But Sigune knew only too well what the outcome would be, if this ignorant lad, unused to the arts of fighting, and armed with nothing better than a short throwing spear, would challenge well-trained fighting men. And so she pointed to a path that would lead Parsifal in the opposite direction — a path that would take him to the lands of King Arthur.

She refused to leave her place in the mountains, she refused to leave her bridegroom's body. She told Parsifal that she had attendants she could call when she wanted them, but that she wished to remain alone with her grief and with her dead knight.

And so Parsifal rode away on the path she had shown him, richer by the name he had now learned, and poorer by the kingdom that should have been his by inheritance and that had been lost.

A few hours later, hunger and tiredness made him look for shelter, and he was glad to find a peasant who, poor as he was, would not refuse hospitality to a lonely stranger. And when Parsifal learned from the man that he was in the realm of King Arthur, everything else — Sigune, the dead knight, his father's kingdom — was forgotten, and he had only one desire: to reach King Arthur's court as soon as possible, and to be made a knight.

And so, the next morning, at his pleading, the peasant took him to the city where King Arthur and the Knights of the Round Table were then in residence.

But when they saw the city before them, the peasant took his leave for, as he said, "The courtiers are all so high and mighty that they would take offence if the likes of me would get near them."

And so, Parsifal, in his fool's garb and on his old mare, rode into King Arthur's city. Having never seen a city, he stared at the houses, at the great number of people in the streets, and hardly noticed that they also stared with amusement at him. Nor was young Parsifal aware that he knew nothing of courtly manners — of any kind of manners. A wild man from far-off mountain forests would have known as much of these things as Parsifal.

But he was blissfully unaware of his ignorance, and so rode on, full of eager expectation, until he reached a meadow — and beyond the meadow, he saw walls girding a great building: the residence of King Arthur. Parsifal's heart beat faster as he saw the place where all his dreams should be fulfilled. But as he looked with shining eyes at the building — far greater than he had ever imagined it — there came a knight, riding out through one of the gates in the wall, and galloping towards Parsifal.

And what a knight he was! His armour was red — as red as a glowing fire — his shield, too, was red as a flame, red were his horse's trappings, and even the horse itself was brown-red in colour. The shaft of his spear, the scabbard of his sword, the reins he held — they were all red.

As the red knight came nearer, Parsifal saw that he carried in one hand a golden goblet, a golden cup. Parsifal was too dumbfounded to find his voice when this splendid red apparition approached. But the red knight reined his horse in, and addressed the speechless youth.

"Blessed be the mother that gave you such good looks. You will find much joy in life, but you will also know grief and pain and sorrow."

Parsifal was hardly prepared for such prophecies, but before he could gather his wits, the red knight continued, "You are on your way to King Arthur, and I charge you to give him a message from me."

"I will, good sir," said Parsifal, with some effort. "What is your message?"

"You must know," said the red knight, "that my name is Ither, and that I lay claim to the lands of King Arthur — they should be mine by rights, and not his. In token of my claim, I have just walked into the hall where Arthur and his knights are taking their meal, and I took this golden goblet that stood, filled with wine, before the king. I took it from the table and, I am sorry to say, as I took it I spilled the wine on Queen Guinevere. But, though I regret the mishap to the Queen, it is but of little account. What matters is that, by ancient custom, he who takes a goblet from a king's table announces thereby his claim to the kingdom — and that is what I have done. Now you go into King Arthur, and tell him that I shall wait here for his best knight to come and fight me for this cup. If I win, the land is mine, and proud Arthur must swear obedience to me as his lord. If I lose, he can keep his cup and his kingdom. Go now, my good lad, and give him this message."

Parsifal, full of wonder about the ways of knights, and full of admiration for the red armour, the whole red outfit of the knight, cried, "I will, Sir Ither!" and rode his horse at its best speed up to the walls of the palace and through a gate and into a forecourt. Here a number of pages stood together, and one of them, Ivanet by name, came and asked him his business.

"My business is with King Arthur," said Parsifal. "Show me the hall where he is at his meal."

"The hall is on the ground floor, and the great arch over there is the entrance," said Ivanet, the page. He might have been less forthcoming with his information if he had known what kind of visitor this was. For Parsifal rode to the entrance and through it and straight into the great hall, where a throng of knights and ladies were sitting at tables, eating and drinking and not a little surprised when a horse and rider appeared in their midst. Parsifal surveyed the great room and the feasting throng calmly from his elevated position, and then said, "God keep you all, brave knights and fair ladies — I give you my greeting, as my mother told me I should."

By now, all faces in the hall were turned towards him, but he continued, quite unabashed, in his clear voice, "I don't know who of you is King Arthur, for you all look like kings to me, but I have a message for him. Ither, the red knight, who took the golden cup, is waiting on the meadow outside for your best knight to fight him for the cup. He is sorry for spilling wine on the queen. And I only wish I had all the red clothes he has on him — they are just what I would like to wear as a knight!"

When he had spoken, there was a great babble of voices in

the hall; the ladies said how handsome he was, the knights said
he looked strong and fit for any fight — but they all wondered if
he was in his right mind, riding into King Arthur's banqueting
hall in a fool's outfit. But then King Arthur raised his voice "I
am the king, and I thank you for the message. The red knight's
insult shall not go unpunished, and every knight of the Round
Table will be eager for the task of dealing with the man who
dares to claim my kingdom."

"No," said Parsifal, to everybody's surprise. "I want the red
knight's armour, I want his horse and weapon — therefore let
me go and fight him."

And then Sir Kay, one of Arthur's knights, shouted furiously,
"You empty-headed young fool, who are you to demand such an
honour? You nitwit — it would serve you right to be knocked
about by the red knight — perhaps he will knock some sense
into your head. Yes — go and fight him, and get his armour ... if
you can!"

But now King Arthur intervened. "Sir Kay, do not speak in
this manner to a youngster whose only fault is his ignorance.
And you, my young friend, do not wish for things that only an
older man with more experience of combat can attain. Forget
about the red knight's splendid armour, and be satisfied with the
one I might give you. Come, dismount from your horse, and
leave the red knight to someone better able to deal with him."

Parsifal, burning with desire for the red armour, and stung
by the insults of Sir Kay, answered, "No, I will not dismount, for
he who waits outside is also on his horse, and I want to ride out
and fight him. And I don't want any other armour or weapon or
horse but his. Give me the red knight's armour, King Arthur!"

"You are as stubborn as you are young and ignorant," said the
king, "but have it your own way. The red armour shall be yours
— if you can get it. And may Heaven protect you, that you suffer no great injury in this foolish attempt."

"Thank you!" cried Parsifal, and turned his horse to ride out.

Now there was a lady in the hall who was a very strange person: she had never laughed in all her life. And there was a saying in
the court of King Arthur that she would laugh, once — and that
would be when she saw the knight who would attain the highest

honour of all. But though she had seen many a great and famous knight — Sir Lancelot, Sir Gawain, and all the other heroes of the Round Table — she had neither laughed, nor even smiled.

But as Parsifal, on his old mare, and in his patched-up fool's outfit, rode through the hall to his encounter with the red knight, he passed the table where this lady was sitting. And she looked at him, and burst out laughing.

Sir Kay, the knight who had been so angry with Parsifal, was sitting next to her. And he saw this woman — who had never laughed before — shaking with laughter at the sight of Parsifal, and he remembered what this laughter meant. He was so furious that he forgot his knightly manners and shouted at her, "You had no laughter or smile for the best knights of this court, and now you laugh at this young nitwit?" And in his fit of temper he did something that was against all rules of knighthood: he struck her in the face.

Parsifal saw it, and stared with astonishment. How could a man, a knight, strike a woman? And then another knight at this table said to him, "She suffers for your sake. Her laughter marked you as the knight who will attain the highest honour. That's why Sir Kay lost his temper."

And Parsifal said, "I cannot wait now to make the man who hurt her and who insulted me pay for his behaviour — unworthy of a knight — but one day he will regret it."

And so he rode out of the palace and to the meadow where Ither, the red knight, was waiting with the golden cup. Behind him there was now the building at which he had looked so expectantly when he came, and where he had met insults and rude behaviour.

As Parsifal turned his head to give a last look at the palace, he saw somebody coming running after him. It was Ivanet, the page, who had first shown him the entrance to the great hall. Of all the people, high and low, in King Arthur's hall, only the page felt enough concern to come along to see how Parsifal would fare at the hands of the red knight.

And so Parsifal, accompanied by the page, rode on to his meeting with the red knight.

The Origins of Knighthood

The men who appear in the Parsifal story are all knights — the whole story begins with young Parsifal's desire to become a knight — and all the motives, all the reasons why people do things, in the story are connected with knighthood.

Now I want to remind you of some things you have heard already — how this institution of knighthood came into existence — that its origin lies in the German tribes which overran and destroyed the Roman Empire.

These Germanic tribes had one outstanding characteristic — a love for fighting, for battle. Whether it was single combat or battle — it was the only thing they lived for.

When a boy was born, the father decided if the baby looked like growing up into a strong warrior. If he thought the child looked ailing or weakly, it was killed. That was the beginning of life — and at the end of life, it was shameful for a man to die in his bed ("straw death" they called it). If a man could not manage to get himself killed in battle, and grew too old, he had himself with all his possessions put on a ship that was set aflame, and he died in the fire, as wind and currents carried the ship away.

These Germanic tribes believed in an afterlife — a life after death. But they imagined that even that life in another world was made enjoyable by battles between the souls of the dead warriors.

So when they went into battle, they threw themselves into the fighting with a wild, savage joy — with a kind of mad fury, which the Romans came to fear, and to know. They called it *Furor Teutonicus,* the Germanic fury.

This "Germanic fury" was in the very blood of these tribes — it was as strong as hunger or thirst, this lust for fighting. Now, such a terrific force or urge does not simply disappear, vanish, in the course of time — it can only be changed, transformed.

And the thing which changed and transformed the Germanic fury, slowly and gradually, was the coming of Christianity. These wild warriors did not, after becoming Christians, simply turn into nice, peaceful citizens — far from it. The first Germanic Christians were as bloodthirsty as their forefathers.

But under the influence of Christianity, this fighting spirit was gradually regulated and made to serve a higher purpose — and so arose the institution of knighthood. A knight was still a fighting man — if there were no battles, knights fought each other in tournaments. But the knight was under an obligation to protect women, the poor and those in distress — he had a duty to keep roads free from robbers, and instead of behaving like a savage, he had to practise courtesy.

In the so-called Dark Ages, when there was no law and order, the knight, the fighting man, became the guardian of the poor and the weak. In this way, Christianity used the wild fighting spirit for a constructive purpose — and civilization, which had disappeared with the fall of Rome, could begin again.

That is why the knights of the Middle Ages mark the beginning of the present civilization.

But the change, the transformation from the savage Germanic fury to the noble and gentle Christian knight was not easily and quickly achieved. You could say that in every knight there lurked, under the courtly manners and high ideals, a savage — a wild, bloodthirsty creature who could break out at any moment.

It was as if in every knight, the dark, old Germanic fury was struggling against the Christian principles — and it was not always that the Christian principles won. You can see it from one of countless historical examples one could give.

During the Hundred Years War between France and England (in 1369), the English king, Edward III, laid siege to the city of Calais. The defenders were willing to surrender — but first they wanted to know what they had to expect if they let the English come into the city. King Edward, who was in a bad mood because he had lost many of his men during the siege, told the messengers from Calais, "I will not spare a single life in your city!"

But this was too much for the English knights who were with him. They entreated the king — they pleaded with him, they reminded him of his knightly vows — and in the end King Edward said reluctantly, "Well, I will spare the population — but six of the leading citizens must be hanged. And that's my last word in this matter."

At this stage, the king's wife, Philippa, who had come to visit him, intervened. She fell on her knees before him, and begged him, for her sake, to spare the six. King Edward stood for a moment frowning and in silence. And then he said, "I wish you were not here today. But as you are here, I cannot refuse your request. The city, and all lives in it, are yours."

In such an episode, you can see how the cruel bloodlust of the Germanic tribes was still there, and was barely held under control by the higher principles of Christianity.

Yet there were also people in those times who achieved, one could say, a miraculous transformation of this fighting spirit. Such a person is, for instance, St Francis of Assisi.

Francis was, to begin with, determined to become a warrior, a knight. He had already taken part in battles, and had fully enjoyed the clash of arms, the feel of danger — the strange intoxication that comes in fighting. But then there came a complete change in his life — as he put it, he felt a call to fight quite a different battle. Against the wishes of his father, he became a monk, and a monk who practised the most extreme forms of self-denial — and a man devoted only to one task: to help those in need.

There is no better illustration than the following story. In the woods near the place where Francis and his followers had settled, there lived a gang of robbers. Three of these robbers, finding themselves short of food, came to the little community, demanding food and brandishing their swords. Francis himself was away at that time, but one of his followers courageously told the robbers what he thought of them. How could they, thieves and murderers, demand food from men of God, who had themselves only collected their scraps by begging? And the robbers, somewhat shamefaced, withdrew. But a little later, Francis returned, and when he heard what had happened, he was furious — with the friar who had sent the robbers packing. It was their duty to think of others first, not of themselves. And a hungry man was a hungry man — robber or not. In the end, the poor friar had to take all the food there was and carry it himself to the hideout of the robbers in the forest.

In Francis, the fighting spirit had, indeed, been transformed into a selflessness and compassion.

This is the thing we have to keep in mind about this age of knights and chivalry — the continuous struggle between the old love for fighting, and the new ideals which Francis of Assisi represented.

And this struggle is by no means over — it goes on right into our times. In the Second World War, most of those who were soldiers killed only because we had to — but I have seen men who positively enjoyed it. They were "throwbacks," men in whom the ancient forces came to light again. And there is still another way in which that old lust for fighting shows itself. There are millions of people who would not dream of committing any act of violence themselves — but what are the films and television shows they like best?

And, of course, if young children are brought up on a mental diet of such shows and films, these old instincts are made stronger, and they grow up with a hunger for violence. It is not surprising if you then hear of teenage gangs fighting battles amongst themselves, of committing crimes for "kicks," of creating havoc just for the fun of it. It is just the old "fury" which is once again breaking loose and hitting out in all directions.

But something else has also happened. The ancient warlust also had its positive side: it was combined with great courage and with a sense of adventure. And as the centuries passed, and Christianity worked on the souls, this courage and sense of adventure led to the Age of Discovery, to the travels of Columbus and Magellan. And still later it became courage and a sense of adventure in the human spirit — and that led to modern science.

The same thing which made us aggressive has also made our science, our inventions, our whole technical progress. On the other hand, there is also the idealism which has led, for instance, to the establishment of the Red Cross.

Henri Dunant, the founder of the Red Cross, was — to begin with — a businessman, a Swiss banker. He went to Paris about some business contract, and he could only get the contract with the agreement of the ruler of France, who was then Napoleon III (a great-nephew of the first Napoleon). But this important man, Napoleon III, was not in Paris. The Italians had asked for his help against the Austrians, and he was in Italy, leading an army. So this Swiss business man, Dunant, travelled to Italy to get his contract signed — and he came just on the eve of a great battle. Napoleon had no time to see him — but Dunant was allowed to stay, and so the next day had a grandstand view of the whole battle from a hill.

This battle, the battle of Solferino, was one of the most murderous battles in history. At the end of the day, when the Austrians were defeated, some 10,000 dead and wounded were left on the battlefield. There were neither doctors nor nurses nor ambulances — not even water for the wounded. All night long, their agonized cries rose from the blood-soaked fields. In that night, the business man, Dunant, forgot his business — he gathered helpers from neighbouring villages, he organized their work and the supplies of water, food, bandages. For three days and nights, the little band worked without rest.

And in these days, Dunant conceived the idea of the Red Cross. He devoted his life to it; his business was ruined by neglect, he lost all he had — but he achieved the Geneva Convention, the establishment of the Red Cross. Then, poor and penniless, he withdrew and lived, unknown, in some valley in Switzerland.

The Red Cross and later organizations like Oxfam are the other side of our inheritance. And both sides go back to the knights of the Middle Ages — the life of a knight was a continuous struggle between these two sides. And we shall see that our hero, Parsifal, had his full share of the aggressive and violent spirit — of the red-hot fury of battle.

The Battle with the Red Knight

You have heard how Parsifal was received at the court of King Arthur. He had found little sympathy for his youthful ardour. The king in his courtly manner, Sir Kay in his rude fashion, had both harped on his youth and lack of experience. The king, out of kindness, wanted to protect him from getting hurt by the red knight. Sir Kay, out of unkindness, had wished him to get hurt, and be taught a lesson by it. Neither had given him a word of encouragement. It is an attitude young people are bound to encounter often in life — and which, like Parsifal, they are bound to resent. But if their heart is set on something — as Parsifal's was set on the red armour — they will go for it just the same, as Parsifal did.

It is in features like this that one can see the great human understanding of the medieval troubadours who composed the story of Parsifal — it is in features like this that the vast gap between our time and their time, our world of mechanical progress and their world of primitive conditions, is bridged. It is features like this which create a link between us and Parsifal, as he rode out to the meadow for his encounter with the red knight.

Ither, the red knight, had put the golden goblet down on a stone, to be ready for the fight as soon as one of Arthur's knights came in answer to his challenge. But it was no knight in armour who now came riding towards him, but the young man he had asked to carry his message. So the red knight asked, "Is none of Arthur's knights coming to fight me for the cup?"

"No," answered Parsifal, "but I asked King Arthur for the splendid red armour you wear, and he said I can have it. So take it off — I can hardly wait to put it on!"

"Listen," said the red knight, "are you quite sure that of all the great knights of the Round Table, none has the courage to fight me?"

But Parsifal was in no mood for explanation. He cried, "Take off your armour — put down your arms! I have told you already they are mine — King Arthur gave them to me."

"That's very generous of him," said the red knight, "he might just as well have given you my life — for you have to take my life first, before you can take my armour."

"It's all the same to me," said Parsifal, who was getting impatient. "If you don't hand the things over willingly, you may well lose your life, as well as the armour! Come on — hand over what King Arthur gave to me!"

The red knight treated the whole thing as a joke, and said, "And by what great deeds have you deserved such a rich reward as my armour?"

"I shall earn what I deserve!" cried Parsifal angrily. "I shall earn it now!" And with these words, he rode close to the red knight and reached over to grab his bridle.

The red knight reversed his spear shaft, and took it in both hands and struck Parsifal with such force that he fell from his horse. Parsifal scrambled to his feet — but as soon as he stood up, there came another glancing blow that tore some skin from his scalp.

In that moment, a blazing fury seized Parsifal — there was a red haze before his eyes, and the blood was pounding in his ears. He saw his throwing-spear lying on the ground, and he quickly picked it up — and with the marksmanship the years in the forest had given him, he sent it straight through the red knight's eye and into the brain.

One moment the tall red figure was upright in the saddle, and the next it came tumbling down to the ground.

In Parsifal's mind there was only room for one thought: "Now the armour is mine — his weapons are mine — his horse is mine!" With clumsy hands, he tore at the helmet, but having no experience with the straps that held a knight's armour together, he could not get it off. He fumbled with the sword belt, but had no better luck.

At this moment, the page, Ivanet, who had watched the

whole encounter, recovered from his amazement at the unexpected outcome. He came running along, and said, "I can hardly believe what I saw — that you brought down a great and famous knight! But let me help you with the armour — you don't know how to handle these things!"

And so, with the page's help, the dead knight was stripped of his armour. Then the page said, "Now, take off the things you are wearing, and put on the fine clothes that go under the armour."

"Oh, no," said Parsifal. "I would not dream of changing the clothes my mother gave me — not for the finest garb in the world!"

And no matter how much the page pleaded with him, Parsifal would not give up his patchwork coat. And so, in the end, Parsifal was encased in the red armour from head to foot, but under it he wore the clothes in which he had come from the forest. He did not know it, but this strange combination was a true picture of himself, who had a knight's outer trappings but not yet the inner aims and obligations that made a true knight.

When Parsifal was at last in full knightly attire and seated on the red horse, he said to Ivanet, "To you, I give the red knight's fine clothes, and the horse that has carried me until now. And take the golden goblet from yonder stone, and bring it back to King Arthur, for I am not going back to his court. I was insulted there by Sir Kay, and a lady was made to suffer for my sake. One day I will come back when I have proved I am as good as any of Arthur's knights, and then the wrong done to the lady will be avenged. Give my greetings to the King!" And with these words, he rode away proudly in his red armour, now he had become the red knight.

The page brought the news and the goblet to King Arthur, and there was great wonder at court that this youngster had slain Ither, a knight of great renown. But Arthur said, "It was not a knightly combat, for knights are forbidden the use of hunting spears when fighting each other. And it was only a stroke of luck that made the throw deadly. In truth, the youngster will not last long — the next knight with experience will make an end of him." To Ither, his dead enemy, King Arthur gave a burial worthy of a great and noble lord.

But as regards Parsifal, the king was mistaken if he thought he would soon lose the new armour and his life — because good luck was with the youngster, and the whole day he met no other knight who might have challenged him to fight.

But towards evening, Parsifal came to a castle, a castle surrounded by great walls and a deep moat with a drawbridge across it. An old man in fine clothes stood on the drawbridge, looking out on the road. Parsifal, as was his habit, said, "Greetings to you, as my mother has told me!"

The old gentleman was puzzled by this strange greeting — he was also puzzled to see a knight in armour of great splendour, who carried his shield and spear in the most clumsy fashion.

And so, driven as much by curiosity as by the rules of hospitality, the old gentleman — Gurnemant was his name — invited Parsifal to be his guest for the night, an invitation which the young man, tired from the unaccustomed weight on him, gladly accepted.

Gurnemant, the host, was not a little surprised when his servants helped the guest out of his armour. Why was the fellow wearing this patchwork garb of a fool? But Gurnemant was too well-mannered to be inquisitive.

Parsifal, however, had no such scruples. For him, the inside of a castle was full of things he had not seen before, and he hardly stopped asking questions from the moment he set foot inside the courtyard.

What were those birds sitting with hoods over their heads in cages? Hunting falcons. Why were there basins with water and towels in the banqueting hall? Because eating with one's hands made the fingers greasy, and so one had to clean them. Why was the tower so high? To see approaching enemies from afar.

He hardly stopped asking questions, until they sat down to their meal. And then old Gurnemant said, "I can see, my young friend, that you know very little of a knight's way of life."

Parsifal admitted candidly that he did not — "but," he added, "I am most anxious to learn."

"Well," said Gurnemant, who had taken a liking to the eager young man, "I am willing to be your teacher — you can stay here and learn from me."

Parsifal was overjoyed by this offer, and told his host how grateful he would be. Then Gurnemant said words which became fateful for Parsifal — more fateful than either he or his host could possibly foresee.

It is often so in life, that a chance word, spoken without any particular intention, can have quite unexpected and far-reaching consequences. Perhaps it is a mercy that we have no foreknowledge of the effects of our words. The words spoken by Gurnemant were certainly going to play a fateful part in Parsifal's life.

What Gurnemant said was this, "As I am to be your teacher, we can start instructions right now. And one of the first rules of courtly manners — of good behaviour — for a knight, is: don't be inquisitive, don't ask too many questions — as you have done since you came. Such questions may, perhaps, embarrass the person you ask — it may also show you up as ignorant — and so, either way, you will not be liked or respected for it."

Gurnemant was well-intentioned when he gave such sound, practical advice to Parsifal — and Parsifal, eager to live up to the rules of knightly conduct, took that advice to heart. Yet, much sorrow was to come from it.

But on that evening, Parsifal told Gurnemant his story — how he had left he forest, how he had learned of the kingdom that should be his by rights, how he had fared at Arthur's court, and how he had gained the red knight's armour. And he learnt that possessing the armour did not make him a knight — that only when he had been trained and instructed would his host, Gurnemant, perform the ceremony called "accolade" which would make him a knight.

And so Parsifal stayed with the noble Gurnemant, and learned the proper use of spear and sword, he learned the rules of knightly combat, and he learned the rules of courtesy. Never had a master a more willing pupil, and so it was not long until the day when Gurnemant touched his shoulder with the flat of the sword and said, "I dub thee — knight!" And when he left the castle, he no longer wore the fool's dress under his armour, he no longer greeted people mentioning his mother, he was no longer ignorant of the ways of the world.

Yet knighthood was not a matter of knowing things, it was a matter of deeds, in strife and battle — in adventure and danger a knight had to prove his worth. And so it was in search of action, in search of foes to be challenged and conquered that Parsifal set out when he left the castle of Gurnemant.

And adventure came to meet him. It was in the late afternoon that he came to a great city. But outside the city there was a camp of armed men — and Parsifal saw they had the long ladders and wooden towers used for the assault of a city. And the city's walls were manned by armed men, ready with bows and arrows and buckets with hot pitch to repel the attackers. The city was besieged. There was, however, no fighting going on, and no-one came to bar his way as he rode past the camp and to the gate of the city. He hammered on the gate, and demanded entry as a stranger who had no part in the quarrel. He was let in, but the men who met him at the gate, all heavily armed, cast dark looks at him and he heard them murmur that, rules of hospitality or not, this was no time to feed a useless visitor.

And coming into the city, Parsifal soon understood the remark. All the people he saw were pale, and mere skin and bones. No smell of cooking came from any house or from the inns — and the stalls in the market place were empty.

From one of the haggard-looking inhabitants, Parsifal learned that the city was under the rule of a young queen, Condwiramur (from French *conduire amour,* to lead to love), and he made his way to her palace.

Even in a city under siege and suffering from starvation, the rules of hospitality for a wandering knight could not be broken, and Condwiramur, the queen, received Parsifal with great courtesy — and with apologies for the meagre fare she could only offer. But Parsifal was hardly aware of whatever food was served to him. From the moment he had set eyes on the queen — who was but a girl of his own age — it was as if suddenly everything else in the world had become unimportant, and the only thing that mattered was to be near her. Thoughtful of his manner, he tried not to stare too obviously at the slim figure, but he could not fail to notice the grave expression on a face which, he thought, was made to smile. And, in his heart, he was already resolved to be "her" knight, to offer his services to her and to do all he could to dispel her troubles.

It was Queen Condwiramur herself who told him of her predicament. The armed men outside the city were the troops of a great and powerful lord who wanted to marry her, and whom she had refused. The proud noble, offended by this refusal, had resorted to force. The siege and the long period of hunger had already worn down the people's will to resist the enemy. But so proud was Kingrun, the rejected suitor, of his strength and skill with arms, that he had offered to withdraw his troops if any of Condwiramur's knights would meet and defeat him in single combat. But none of her knights, weakened as they were by hunger, had dared to accept the challenge.

When Condwiramur finished her tale, her eyes met with Parsifal's, and what he read in the glance was both a request and a promise. And if, in that moment, Condwiramur had asked him to fight the Lord of Hell, he would have undertaken the task happily. But fighting a mere mortal for her sake was a pleasure, a joy, the very thing he longed to do. When he promised Condwiramur to fight Kingrun in single combat, he felt happier than at any time since he had left the forest.

When the great lord Kingrun was told that one of Condwiramur's knights had accepted his challenge, he thought of the combat as a pleasant interlude in the tedious business of laying siege to the city. He had never met his equal in battle or tournament, and looked forward to claiming another victim to his strength and skill. It was a combat that was watched from both sides — anxiously from the walls of the city, eagerly from the encircling camp.

From a great distance, the two knights began to ride against each other. First slowly, then faster and faster, the horses covered the distance between them, and the knights held their long spears "at rest" pointing at each other's shield. And, in the middle, at full gallop, they crashed into one another with such force that both spears broke, and the horses sank to their haunches. Both knights dismounted as quickly as the heavy armour would permit, and drew their swords, and struck at each other. Their shields were hacked to pieces, but they still fought on, exchanging blow for blow. But by now Kingrun, who had been so confident of his strength, began to feel the strain — his sword-arm began to feel as heavy as lead ... and then Parsifal struck Kingrun's helmet with such force that the blow sent Kingrun staggering, and a second blow sent him crashing to the ground. The next moment, the point of Parsifal's sword was at Kingrun's throat — in the space between helmet and body-armour.

"Go on — kill me!" croaked the fallen man. "I would have done it to you!"

"I give you another choice," said Parsifal. "You have to swear to obey two conditions. One is that the siege of the city is lifted — and the other condition is that you betake yourself to the court of King Arthur, and place yourself at the service of the lady who was struck in the face for my sake. And give King Arthur greetings from the red knight!"

Kingrun was not such a fool as to throw his life away — he swore to abide by the conditions. And so Parsifal returned as victor to Condwiramur. And it will surprise no-one to hear that he married her, and became king of the city called Belrepeire. He was happy — but the real trials of his life were still to come. He had his share of good fortune, but had yet to learn the lessons of grief and sorrow.

Arthur — Myth or History?

The stories about King Arthur and his knights contain, of course, a good deal of fighting — war, battle, tournament, joust, single combat — and we know already that there are historical reasons for this interest in strife and violence. It is quite in keeping with the general spirit of those times that the part I told you yesterday began with the killing of the red knight and ended with the combat outside the city of Queen Condwiramur.

But there is not only all the fighting of the knights of King Arthur — there is also another great fight, another great battle connected with King Arthur, and this other battle is not fought with spears and swords, but with pen and paper, and what's more, it is not a battle of the past, it goes on right into the present. It is the question of whether King Arthur and his knights ever really existed or are pure invention.

You will probably be inclined to think that the King Arthur stories are no more "real" or "true" than the story of Red Riding Hood. But it is not quite so simple.

You see, the question "King Arthur — man or myth?" as it is usually put, is rather like a detective story, with clues all over the place — and the only difficulty is to read these clues correctly.

One set of clues is the many places all over Britain and northern France which are, by local tradition, connected with King Arthur — the ruin of Tintagel Castle in Cornwall, or Glastonbury Abbey, or Arthur's Seat in Edinburgh. There is such a wealth of local traditions about Arthur here and there all over Britain that it does not seem likely it all came from nothing, from sheer invention.

But, on the other hand, there was certainly no King Arthur and no Knights of the Round Table at the time when the troubadours wrote all these stories. But the troubadours did not make it all up. They used stories which existed already. Long before the troubadours, there were story-tellers in every village in Britain who spoke of Arthur and his heroes. Neither the bards nor their audience could read or write, but by word of a mouth the stories were kept alive from generation to generation. King Arthur was a British hero long, long before the troubadours wrote down the stories — and they took great liberties with them. The troubadours made Arthur and his men behave like knights of their own time — they dressed them up in the costumes of the twelfth and thirteenth century. But the stories of Arthur and Gawain and Lancelot existed already — the troubadours only "adapted" the stories, added something here and there — they did not "invent" King Arthur.

The troubadours chose Arthur and his men because they were already popular heroes — because people wanted to hear more and more of them — they were already known and loved by the British people. For the people of Britain, King Arthur was already then — around 1100–1200 — not just one of the British kings, he was *the* king — the embodiment of the true spirit of Britain. This was and still is today the importance of King Arthur: that in the hearts of the people he remained the hero who stood for the spirit of Britain, for all that is British in the highest and best sense.

But, you see, this is where the battle over King Arthur is still going on: were these early stories told only by word of mouth just fantasy, a myth? Or did they go back to a real person, a king who once lived and whose fame was never forgotten?

But there is still a third possibility. There is a school of thought which maintains that there is an answer which makes Arthur a man and a myth at the same time. They say that "Arthur" was not the name of a person, but the title given to the leader of a special group of men who lived far back in Celtic times — when one leader died, his successor became "Arthur." And so there were many Arthurs, not just one.

For many generations, this group — the heroes of the Round Table — led by their "Arthur," worked and strove to protect the weak in those barbaric times; they devoted themselves to the task of fighting against oppression, cruelty, of holding robbers and brutal power at bay — they stood against all the evils of a cruel and savage time: they were "knights" before there was knighthood. It was a kind of "brotherhood" — very probably a secret brotherhood, and very likely a brotherhood with branches all over Britain, with each branch having its own leader, its own "Arthur."

This is the third opinion, the third view about the origin of the Arthur stories: this third view has the advantage that all the clues fit, and that it explains why the memory of Arthur and his heroes was so dear to the people of Britain — and why they saw in Arthur a symbol of what is best in the British: a sense of what is fair and just, and the courage to fight for it.

And when, many centuries later, the knights of the Middle Ages followed the same ideals, what better model, what better example, could they find than the Arthur whom people still remembered? No wonder the troubadours, who were themselves knights, took up the ancient Celtic stories and made all their knights servants of Arthur.

The real Arthurs, the Celtic leaders, must have lived well before Christianity reached Britain — they followed the Druid religion, which was a worship of the sun. But by protecting the weak and the poor, by fighting against cruelty and brutality, they were already working for Christian ideals, for Christian principles.

And the strange thing is that when the first Christian missionaries did come to the Celtic people of the British Isles, it was as if these people had only been waiting for it — the new religion was readily accepted. It was as if the Arthurs had prepared the way for it. So, when the troubadours in their stories made Arthur a Christian king, they were not so far out, because there was something Christian in the Arthur of olden times.

So, you see, although the stories about King Arthur and his knights do contain a good deal of fantasy, of sheer invention, of fairy tales, it is *not* all fantasy, and there is, far in the background, something that really happened.

It is like the story of the Trojan War, which was also for a long time regarded as a myth, until Schliemann dug up the ruins of Troy — still blackened by the fire that had destroyed the city.

And you know — even the fantastic parts of the Arthur stories, the parts which seem no more than fairy tales, are not quite so unreal, so wildly imaginative as it may seem at first sight. Let's take the very beginning of the story of King Arthur. We are told in the story that when Arthur's father, King Uther Pendragon, died, there was confusion and chaos in Britain, for Arthur was still only a babe, and the powerful lords fought each other for the throne.

Merlin, the wizard and guardian of the child, took the little Arthur to foster parents who were willing to look after the boy and to bring him up — but Merlin did not tell them who the boy was, nor did the boy himself know it.

The foster father was himself a knight, Sir Ector, and he took part in the struggle for the crown of Britain. But all the fighting led to nothing — none of the contenders could gain a decisive victory over his competitors. And after many years of this fruitless strife amongst themselves, the lords decided to find by peaceful means who should be king of Britain.

And now Merlin, the wizard, took a hand again. At his advice, the highest priest in Britain, the Archbishop of Canterbury, called all the lords to a meeting in London at Christmas. At this meeting, a sign would be given as to which of them was worthy to wear the crown of Britain. They all came to London, and a great service was held in which they all prayed that the right person should be chosen.

When they came out of the church, they saw a strange sight in the churchyard — it was a great square stone, and in the stone was an anvil, and through the anvil and stone there was a sword. And there was an inscription on the sword. It read: "He who can pull this sword from the stone is the rightful king of Britain."

Of course, each one of the lords in turn tried to pull the sword out of the anvil and stone, but not one of them was able to move it an inch. And when they turned in bewilderment to the Archbishop, he said: "It seems that the right man is not yet amongst us. We must wait for his coming."

To pass the time of waiting, the lords decided to arrange a tournament amongst themselves. Now, amongst the nobles who had come to this meeting there was Sir Ector, the foster father of Arthur, and with him was his son, whose name was Kay, and also young Arthur. Kay, the son of Sir Ector, had already been knighted a short time before — and Arthur, being only a foster brother and of unknown parentage, was the young knight's servant and page.

When all the nobles were making ready for the tournament, the young knight, Kay, said to Arthur, "When we left our lodging in town this morning, I left my sword behind, as I did not expect a tournament. Go quickly, and bring it to me."

Arthur hurried back to the lodging — but everybody in the house had gone out, the doors were locked and he could not get in. What should he do? Kay would be very cross if he came without the sword. But as Arthur made his way back, he passed the now deserted churchyard with the stone and the sword through it. Here was a sword! And without thinking twice, Arthur went over, pulled the sword out without difficulty and brought it to his master.

Arthur, who could not read, and had paid little attention to the affairs of the high and mighty lords, had no idea that there was anything special about the sword. But young Sir Kay recognized immediately the sword and the inscription, and he realized what had happened. But the temptation of holding this precious sword in his hands was too much for him. He went to his father, Sir Ector, and said, "Look — here is the sword from the stone! I am to be King of Britain." But Sir Ector was not easily deceived. Under his questioning, Kay had to admit, blushing with shame, that it was Arthur who had given him the sword.

And then Arthur, much to his surprise, accompanied by all the lords, had to go back to the stone in the churchyard, and there, before all of them, he put the sword into the stone and drew it out again — but none of the others could do it. And so, in the end, Arthur became King of Britain.

This is the story of the famous sword "Excalibur," the "Sword in the Stone." Now, the storytellers of those times — the bards first, and the troubadours later — used such imaginative pictures as symbols: they wanted to convey by this story that Arthur alone possessed something which all the others did not have — and they compared this "something" to a sword, the sword Excalibur. And only this "something" made a man worthy like a leader, a king.

What is there in a man's character that would qualify him for leadership? Is it the inner strength to make decisions — and right decisions

Just compare the two words "incision" and "decision": *incision* means a cut, and *decision* also has "-cision," which means cutting. A firm decision is a cut. And the sword Excalibur is the power to make decisions — the right decisions.

We have in more recent times an example of this power of decision. In 1940, the armies of Hitler overran France — the French armies were in full flight, and the French Government surrendered France to German occupation. The British troops who had been fighting in France had been safely brought back to England by the Dunkirk evacuation — but they had lost all their arms. Britain was practically defenceless against a German invasion — and had obviously no other choice but to do what France had done: surrender to Hitler. Both in Parliament and amongst the people, there were many who thought that all we could do was to try and get tolerably good peace terms from Hitler — the war was lost.

And then came Winston Churchill's famous broadcast, in which he told the world that, under his leadership, Britain would fight on — and would never surrender to Hitler. It was one man's decision, one man's determination which, in those bleak days of 1940, saved Britain and the world from Nazi domination.

But if one of the old troubadours had heard Churchill's voice in 1940, and if he had witnessed the Battle of Britain, when the RAF defied Hitler's Luftwaffe, that troubadour would have said, "The sword Excalibur has been drawn from the stone — Winston Churchill has the power of Excalibur!"

The bards in very ancient times, and the troubadours of the Middle Ages, spoke a language of symbolic pictures, where we in our time use abstract words, such as "decision," without realizing that "decision" was from a Latin word which means "to cut" — and so in the word itself there is already the picture of a knife or sword.

But once we understand that seemingly fantastic stories have a meaning, that they illustrate something in pictures, we can also understand such an apparently absurd story as is told about the end of King Arthur — that he has not died, but rests in a kind of sleep in "Avalon," and will return to Britain in her hour of greatest need. When the little ships of England sailed out against the Armada — when Nelson in the Battle of Trafalgar foiled Napoleon's invasion plans — when, in the Battle of Britain, a pitiful few RAF planes stood up to Hitler's Luftwaffe — these were all hours of need, and in all these hours of need there rose the spirit which once lived in all the Arthurs. In ordinary times, when there is no danger, one might well think that there is no spirit in the British, that it is dead. But it is only under a spell — as Arthur is said to be held in a spell in Avalon. And this spirit has risen every time there was a dire need.

So, you see, all these seemingly fantastic stories — the "Sword in the Stone," or that Arthur did not die but only lies asleep under a magic spell — are not idle fancy, they have a hidden meaning.

8

The Fisher King

Parsifal had been accompanied by good fortune, without quite realizing it. It was good fortune which had helped him against the red knight. It was good fortune which had brought him to Gurnemant, who had given him the training and instructions necessary for a knight. And it was good fortune which had brought him to Queen Condwiramur — and in one fight he had earned her hand in marriage and the crown of a king.

He had been very fortunate indeed — and he lived in great happiness with Queen Condwiramur. But as time passed, he thought more and more often of his mother, Herzeloyde. He did not know that she had died of grief in the very hour he had left the forest — and now that he had achieved knighthood and gained a kingdom he wished that his mother should be with him to share his happiness.

It would not do to send a messenger — no, he himself would go, tell her how well he had fared, and bring her back with him from the solitude of the forest to his palace.

He was loath to part from his wife, but he had a duty towards his mother, and so there came the day when he took leave of Queen Condwiramur and set out on his journey to the great forest where he had spent his early youth.

He rode for a day, but as evening came he found himself in a region quite unknown to him. There were hills, the slopes of which were covered with dense woods, there were lakes — but nowhere could he see any sign of human habitation. Was there any place where he could find shelter for the night?

No knight's castle or peasant's hut could be seen, and so Parsifal rode on, and came to one of the lakes he had seen gleaming between the hills. And, as he was glad to see, there were people whom he took to be fishermen. There was a boat on the lake, and several people in it. Parsifal hailed them, and the boat came towards him.

As the boat approached, he could make out that there was one man in it who was dressed in splendid robes of purple and ermine, such as only a great lord or a king would wear; the other men in the boat seemed to be servants.

Nearer came the boat, and now Parsifal could see that the face of the noble lord or king was pale, and bore the mark of great suffering. When Parsifal asked him where he could find shelter, the sad-looking man said, "For thirty miles around, there is no house, except one that is nearby. At the end of yonder cliff, you will find an uphill path. Follow that path, and you will reach a castle. I myself will be your host there tonight, when I have done with fishing in the lake."

Parsifal thanked the man whom he called in his mind the "Fisher King," and followed the directions given to him. The path up the hill was steep and winding, and more than once he thought of turning back, for he could see no sign of a castle, and began to wonder if he had not been sent on a fool's errand. But, just as the sun set, he saw in the golden glow of the dusk over the trees the towers of a castle. There was a great moat around the castle, but as Parsifal approached, a drawbridge was let down, and the gate was opened to receive him.

Pages and squires came to meet him in the forecourt, and when Parsifal told them the Fisher King had sent him, they bade him welcome. They helped him from the saddle, they led him to a chamber in the castle where they helped him out of his armour, they brought hot water and towels to clean himself, and a silken coat to put on in place of his travel-stained clothes.

All this was the kind of hospitality one would expect from the house of a rich and noble lord. But, in one way, there was something strange and unusual about this castle. There was none of the laughter and shouting that one would hear in any castle — no-one hummed a song, or whistled, and even the pages acted with the gravity of old men and not like young boys. Knights or squires or pages — they all showed Parsifal every courtesy, but there was no smile on any face, and they all seemed weighed down with some great sorrow or unhappiness.

Parsifal wondered what was the matter with them — and what was the matter with the lord of the castle, whose pale, suffering face he could not forget. But he well remembered the instructions of his teacher, Gurnemant: a knight must not be inquisitive, he must not ask too many questions. And, in any case, if these people had troubles, it was of no concern to him. And so he asked no questions — and when he was ready, he was led to the banqueting hall.

It was a more lordly hall than Parsifal had ever seen — even King Arthur had nothing to equal it. Chandeliers with hundreds of wax candles spread soft light — in three great fireplaces logs gave warmth as well as a pleasant scent. Along the walls were many couches on which knights rested, and by each couch stood a table.

Raised above the others was the place of honour — and it was occupied by the Fisher King. Although the hall was well heated, he wore a robe of fur, and seemed to shiver in it. He said to Parsifal, "Forgive me that I don't stand up to greet you — but, believe me, this is not lack of courtesy that prevents me. Please take your seat beside me."

Parsifal had hardly sat down, when a page appeared before the Fisher King, carrying a sword with a golden hilt, and in a jewel-encrusted sheath. The host took the sword and gave it to Parsifal. "It is for you, my honoured guest," he said. "It will serve you well — it will never break, except in one danger — what this danger is, is only known to the master who made the sword."

Parsifal was still stammering his thanks for the precious gift when he became aware that all talking in the great hall had ceased. He, too, fell silent, and in the hush a side door opened, and in came a man carrying a long spear in his hand. The man carried the spear through the hall, and Parsifal saw to his amazement that the point of the spear was red with blood and that drops spattered on the floor as the man walked through and, finally, went out by another door.

Deep sighs could be heard — but not a word was spoken, and Parsifal was greatly puzzled to know what it all meant. But he wondered even more about what followed.

For now entered a lady, followed by two pages: she carried in her hands a vessel — it seemed a crystal — that shone so brightly that all the other lights in the hall seemed pale and wan. And Parsifal heard a whisper: "The Grail ..."

And as this thing, called "Grail," was carried by the lady round the hall, a great number of pages placed golden bowls before every guest — and then the strangest of all things came to pass. For, as the Grail was carried past the tables, each bowl was filled with the food the guest wished, that he liked best.

Parsifal, too, found the golden plate before him filled with food that no-one had served — and as he saw all the others eating, he too helped himself. And when they had all eaten, the lady with the thing called "Grail" left.

By now, Parsifal felt very curious indeed — but he also remembered the rule not to show curiosity. What would his host think of him if he showed such bad manners as to ask questions? And so he kept silent.

When the meal was over, the host said, with a deep sigh, "I think your bed is ready — you must be tired after your long journey, so I advise you to go and rest." Parsifal rose, thanked the host once again for the gift of the sword and, wishing him a good night, left. All other knights, too, rose, and some came to show him to his room.

Parsifal was, indeed, tired, but he was also bewildered by what he had seen. And now that he was alone, he could also feel a strange premonition of distress. It followed him even in his sleep, for his night was disturbed by nightmare dreams — he felt himself pierced by swords, and trampled under horses. With a groan, he woke up, covered in sweat — but he was glad to see that it was already daylight. He expected that at any moment pages would appear to help him with his armour. But no-one came.

"Have they all been called away to fight an enemy?" thought Parsifal. "They could at least have told me — I would gladly have helped them!" But it was no use speculating, and no use waiting any longer. He got up and put on his clothes and, with some trouble, got into his armour. There was the sword he had once taken from the red knight, as well as the precious blade he had received from the Fisher King. He put them both on, and left his room.

There was still not a soul to be seen in the castle, so Parsifal went out into the courtyard. There he saw his horse tethered to a post, and his spear and shield leaning against the post. He knocked at some doors and windows, but there was no answer. "Well," he thought, "they don't expect me to say goodbye, it seems, but they have put things ready for my departure, so I will be on my way."

He mounted and rode towards the gate. The drawbridge was down, and Parsifal rode over it — but before he had come to the end of the bridge, somebody behind began to pull it up, so that Parsifal's horse had to jump to clear the gap. Parsifal turned round furiously, and shouted, "What manners are these — not letting me ride to the end of the bridge?"

And in answer came a voice from the ramparts of the castle, "Ride on, fool! You were too stupid to use your mouth for anything but gulping food last night — and a curse on you for not asking what you should have asked!"

It was a shock for Parsifal that from people who had been so courteous the day before there should now come rudeness and curses. He shouted, "What do you mean by all this? What question should I have asked?" But there was again silence, and no-one answered his shouting. And Parsifal felt again that dark foreboding which had been with him all night.

Upset and unhappy without knowing why, Parsifal spurred his horse and went down the winding path which had brought him up to the castle the night before. Soon he reached the cliff where the path began — and then he was again in that region where no human habitation could be seen for miles. But as he rode on, the countryside became more familiar to him — surely he had passed this little stream, and that mountain, when he rode from the forest to King Arthur's court? He must be getting nearer to the great forest, and to his mother.

And then, turning a bend, he came upon a sight he had seen before — a woman with a dead knight. Surely it could not be his cousin, Sigune, who had once told him his name? But as he came nearer he could see that it was Sigune. But she looked aged by many years, she was dressed in black — and the dead man lying in a coffin at her feet was embalmed.

And the woman, too, recognized Parsifal. She said, "Don't be surprised, cousin, to find me here! I have sworn to stay with my dead lover until my own life comes to an end. But if there is one thing that can bring joy to me in my grief, it is the sight of the new sword on your side. I know this sword, and it tells me that you have been to the Fisher King."

"Yes," said Parsifal. "He gave it to me!"

"Dear cousin," cried Sigune with joy, "you have been to the castle Montsalvage, the castle of salvation. You are indeed blessed, for you have seen the holy Grail!"

"Well, " said Parsifal, "I did not know the castle was called Montsalvage, but I saw some strange things there."

"Surely," said Sigune, "you have asked the question — the question that brings the highest honour there is in the world?"

"Question?" said Parsifal. "No, I did not ask any question!"

"You wretch!" cried the woman. "You saw that ailing, suffering man, the Fisher King, and you felt no pity, no compassion that would make you ask what was his hurt, or why he was ailing?"

"It would not have been fitting for a knight ..." stammered Parsifal.

"Not fitting?" cried Sigune. "You fool, you wretched fool! If you had thought less about what is fitting, and if you had a spark of pity in your heart, you would have gained honour beyond your dreams. Know, then, that it was ordained by that which is called the Grail that the Fisher King, who did a great wrong, shall suffer from a painful wound until a knight comes who will — out of himself, and unbidden — ask: 'Why are you ailing?' And as soon as that question is asked, the Fisher King's wound would be healed, and the knight who asked the question would be rewarded with the highest honour in the world. But you, in your dumbness and in your pride and in your cold-heartedness — you, for whom the Fisher King and his whole company of knights of the Grail have been waiting — you have kept silent, and so you have lost the greatness that was to be yours! And, having failed to ask, you are cursed. A curse is on you — go away, accursed one, and leave me alone!"

"But, cousin Sigune," said Parsifal, "for me the place was only a night's shelter ... I am on my way back to my mother in the forest, and I gave little thought to anything else!"

"To your mother?" said Sigune. "You will have to seek her in Heaven. She died of a broken heart the day you rode away, thinking of nothing else but your own glory as a knight. You thought only of yourself when you left your mother — you thought only of yourself when you kept silent before the Fisher King, and so you have lost your mother, and you have lost your place amongst the knights of the holy Grail!" To Parsifal, every word she spoke was like a shattering blow. His mother dead — and he had caused her death ... a curse on him — and he had caused the curse! His mind could not grasp it.

At long last, he said, "I cannot bring my mother back to life again — but I can at least go back to the Grail Castle, to Montsalvage, and ask the question I did not ask the first time."

And Sigune looked up and said, "Poor Parsifal — no-one can find the castle of the Grail by seeking for it. Only the Grail itself guides those who are meant to find Montsalvage — all others can never find it. It was given to you from birth, by the noble blood you have inherited — it was your precious inheritance to find the Grail Castle, but you have forfeited this inheritance."

Without a word, Parsifal turned his horse and rode back the way he had come. He remembered well every mile he had travelled that day, and he was determined to find that cliff and that path winding uphill through the woods to the castle.

For hours he explored every hill, for hours he searched for that lake on which he had seen the fishermen — but he found neither lake nor cliff nor path. It was as if it all had been a dream, which had left no trace.

Manichaism and Albigenses

Parsifal's meeting with the Fisher King is — like the sword of King Arthur — a picture, a symbolic picture, and is not to be taken as a physical event. But these pictures — the ailing Fisher King, the castle Montsalvage, the thing called the "Grail" — are not as easily explained or interpreted as King Arthur's sword. These pictures of the castle Montsalvage and the holy Grail are, one could say, a message, a last message sent by men who saw their world destroyed by evil forces — a message they sent out, so that in the future their most sacred beliefs should not be forgotten. But the message had to be put into such a form that the enemies would not recognize it, and would let it pass. The Grail story is a picture, a symbolic picture, in which a certain group of people, threatened with destruction, sent a message to the humankind of the future.

You know that in the early centuries of the Middle Ages the Roman Catholic Church was all-powerful, and that it suppressed ruthlessly any "heresies" — which means any ideas which did not conform with the "dogma" of the Church. "Dogma" means the official teaching of the Church. To be a "heretic," to express any view forbidden by "dogma," was to invite torture and death at the stake. Nevertheless, there were "heresies," there were people who dared to defy the Church. In the twelfth century, around 1100, one particular heresy had found large support in the south of France, in Provence. The people who followed this heresy were called "Albigenses."

The Albigenses in the south of France were so numerous that there were practically no Roman Catholics left amongst them. They had their own churches, their own priests, their own Bible. Nobles and merchants and peasants — every class had taken up this heresy. And while the rest of Europe was still in the "Dark Ages," the Albigenses in Provence had reached a flourishing civilization — poetry and the arts flourished amongst them.

And — something quite unheard of in those days — they preached tolerance towards any form of religion. Jews and Muslims could live unmolested and undisturbed amongst them — in fact, they had very cordial relations with the Arabs in Spain.

All this was, of course, a thorn in the flesh of the Church of Rome. If this sort of thing was allowed to go on, the heresy might spread to other lands — in fact, it was already spreading. And so Pope Innocent III in Rome called for a "Crusade" — not a crusade against Turks or Muslims, but against Christians, the Albigensians.

And he found volunteers for this crusade: some, no doubt, came from religious fanaticism, but most of them came in the hope of plunder from the rich cities of Provence. And thus came the"Albigensian Crusade" cam about.

People in the Middle Ages were generally cruel and blood-thirsty, but the bestiality of that Albigensian Crusade was, even for those days, hair-raising. City after city went up in flames, whole populations were massacred and those who died quickly were the lucky ones.

The last Albigensians took refuge in a castle in the Pyrenees, Montségur. When this last refuge was surrounded by the "Crusaders," it was only a matter of time until the end came. After surrendering, the remaining Albigenses were dragged down the mountain path from the castle. Rather than re-nouncing their beliefs, men, women and children chose to be burned alive in one great fire. And so the Albigensian heresy was wiped out.

But there was still an Albigensian "underground" movement (as we would call it), a movement which worked in two ways, to keep their cherished beliefs alive. One way was the troubadours: many of the troubadours were secretly Albigenses, and they used their art, their poetry, to express in a veiled from — in a form the Roman Church would not recognize — the faith and the knowledge which the so-called "Crusade" had removed from the earth.

The stories of King Arthur and his knights had already been popular, and now the troubadours — or, rather, some of them — added a new feature to these stories: they introduced the story of the Grail and the Knights of the Grail.

So the Grail story is a veiled expression of a kind of Christianity which was not allowed to live openly and which was at that time brutally suppressed and persecuted as a heresy. And this brings us to the question: what was the Albigensian heresy? In which way was it different from the Roman Church, or any Church which exists today?

And to find an answer to this question, we must go back in history, very far back, to about four thousand years before our present time.

About four thousand years ago, there spread in the Middle East, in the region which is now called Iran or Persia, a remarkable religion. This religion saw the whole world, the universe, earth and man himself, involved in a great war between the powers of light and the powers of darkness. Light did not mean just physical light, but also the hosts of all that is good and wholesome in the world, and darkness was not mere physical darkness but the visible expression of all that is evil and corrupting in the world. The Lord of the hosts of light was called Ahura Mazda, and the Lord of the powers of darkness was Ahriman.

The people of ancient Persia regarded every human being as involved in this great cosmic strife. Every human deed helped either one side or the other — the light or the darkness. And the ancient Persians felt themselves as servants of the Kingdom of Light, and all their work here on earth was in the service of the Lord of Light.

This religion had very far-reaching, practical results. The Persians, for instance, were able to change a kind of wolf into a useful domestic animal, the dog. By this transformation of a savage beast into man's faithful friend, they had gained a victory over the powers of darkness. Far more important was another "transformation" — they changed a kind of wild grass into the first kind of cereal, and all our wheat and oats and barley are descendants of this original plant, cultivated four thousand years ago. The whole of agriculture began four thousand years ago in this region, and then spread to Asia and to Europe. The Persians were also the first to change wild roses into garden roses, and wild trees into the fruit trees we have now.

Now, when I say they "changed" wild trees, it sounds much simpler than it really is. If you take the seeds of a sweet, juicy apple and plant them, the tree you grow will not bear any apples you could eat — they will only be wild apples, "crab apples." If you want eating apples, you must "graft" a twig of a good apple tree on to a young, new wild tree. Once there is a tree bearing sweet apples, any amount of wild trees can be changed by grafting. And it is the same with every fruit tree, and with every rose. But how did the Persians get their first tree bearing sweet apples — the first bush with garden roses? That is what we do not know, and it is still beyond present-day science. Even our most advanced methods cannot change a crab apple without grafting.

So this religion of ancient Persia had immense practical consequences — it changed man from a hunter and a nomad, to a settled life as a farmer — it made cities and civilization possible.

And then centuries passed — the Persians became decadent, and their religion degenerated to a formality. Christianity came — but it made very few converts in Persia. Then, about AD 300, a Persian, Mani, founded a new religion, a kind of synthesis between the religion of Persia and Christianity. He spoke of Christ as the Lord of Light, who had come to earth to help man in the struggle against the powers of darkness.

But there was a significant change in the teaching of Mani. First of all, this war between light and darkness was not like human wars which aim at the destruction of the enemy. When Christ, the King of Light, gains a victory over evil, that evil is transformed, changed into a higher good. In every evil, there is hidden a higher force for good which lies, as it were, enchanted in it — waiting to be awakened and released. And the second change was that Mani put the emphasis on changes in man himself, not on changing animals or plants. What is savage and wild in the soul has to be transformed to become a power for good.

This teaching of Mani made him enemies amongst the Persians and the Christians. The Persians were against him for bringing new ideas into their religion, and the Christians were horrified at the idea of regarding evil as something that could be redeemed and transformed. In the end, Mani was executed by order of the king of Persia.

But Mani had already found followers — they were called "Manicheans." These Manicheans were expelled from Persia — but the Christian countries of Europe gave them no better welcome. They were accused of worshipping evil and persecuted. Yet, in spite of this, the Manichean teaching spread, particularly in southern France, in Provence.

And the Albigenses belonged to this stream. Their heresy was the heresy of Mani. The destruction of the Albigenses was only the last chapter in a long story of persecution.

This Albigensian heresy still carried the stamp of its Persian origin — they still spoke of the "Kingdom of Light" and the "Kingdom of Darkness." And Wolfram, the troubadour, speaks as a Manichean, as a follower of Mani, when he lets the mother say to Parsifal, about God:

> Son, He is brighter than the day
> And, once, to help man on his way
> He lived as man on earth indeed.
> To Him you turn in every need.
> But dark is he who by his art
> Makes men from God's true ways depart.

It is a Manichean picture of the Kingdom of Light and the Kingdom of Darkness.

The Manicheans, the Albigenses spoke about "darkness" and "light" in the human soul. We, today, do not use these words — we use a different terminology. We now have a science called "psychology," the science of the soul. And the psychologists have discovered that, besides the conscious mind, there is also a "subconscious" part of the soul. A great part of our soul is immersed in darkness and we are, normally, not aware of what goes on in this darkness of the subconscious. But it does happen, in certain cases, that something "erupts" from the depths of the subconscious into the conscious mind — we call such an eruption a "neurosis." Some psychologists made a special study of such cases, for these "eruptions" can give an indication of what goes on in the darkness of the subconscious. The two great names in the science of the subconscious are Freud and Jung. There is still a great controversy going on about the merits of either school of thought — but one thing is quite certain: *that in this darkness of the subconscious we carry — each one of us, no matter how good we are in our conscious behaviour — in the subconscious a host of evil, destructive inclinations.*

Normally we are spared a knowledge of this hell in our subconscious, but if there is a crack in the dam which keeps the evil forces down, when they rise they can destroy the whole human personality. I am afraid these cases are on the increase, they are becoming more frequent. The psychiatrists who have to deal with these patients are faced with a great problem. There are useful drugs, but the drugs are not a cure — they only suppress the symptoms. *A real cure could only consist in changing, in transforming these evil, destructive forces which come to the surface into something positive, something good and wholesome.*

So, you see, modern psychology, modern psychiatry, is faced with the same problem that occupied the Manicheans, the Albigenses. We do not use the same words, we do not use the same terminology, but the modern psychologist (who may not believe in God — or Christ — or the Kingdom of Light) is faced with the problem of the Manicheans and the Albigenses. He is faced with the problem of changing, transforming the evil that is boiling up from the subconscious of his patient.

Now Professor Freud, who was the first to investigate these dark forces, coined a word for this change, for this transformation that is necessary to save the mental balance of the patient — he called it "sublimation." The task of the doctor would be to help the patient to "sublimate" the dark urges of the subconscious.

Freud coined the word "sublimation," but, in practice, it happens very rarely indeed that it is possible to bring about such a "sublimation." In the rare cases where it did happen, it is not even known why this particular patient succeeded. Professor Jung, the other great name in analytical psychology, maintained that patients with strong religious convictions stood a much better chance than others. He regarded religion as a decisive creative force.

And now we can go back to the Albigenses. They were well aware of that dark part of the human soul — they did not need neuroses to make them aware of it. They said: this dark and evil element in us is not here by accident — it is in our organization, in the body, in the blood. The blood that circulates in the body was for them not merely a physical substance, but also the physical carrier of emotions, passions, instincts, desires, including the dark urges of the subconscious. And they spoke of something that can work right into the blood, right into the depths of the subconscious, and can transform the evil and destructive urges into powers for good, into wholesome forces, and that is what they called "the holy Grail."

In the first chapter we saw that modern science is concerned with the secrets of matter while the ancient mysteries were concerned with the secrets of the spirit. Mani and his followers, the Manicheans, the Albigenses, were concerned with a third kind of secret — the secrets of the soul. How can the conscious mind change and transform the subconscious? How can the subconscious evil be transformed into good?

You see, if we human beings were only physical matter, a kind of complicated machine, there would be no question of good and evil — machines have no moral problems. If we were only pure spirits, there would also be no question of good or evil — we would be good without any possibility of evil. But, as souls, we stand in between spirit and matter, and are faced with moral decisions. In our conscious mind, we would always want to do the right thing, but our subconscious sends out urges and promptings which interfere with our good moral intentions.

Normally we can keep these subconscious forces in check, we can control them. The criminal, the murderer is a person who cannot control them. But the Manicheans set out to do more than just controlling the subconscious — their aim was to transform it. And that spiritual power that can work into the subconscious, into the organic processes which send up the blind urges and promptings, this power they called the "Grail."

In the story, the word "Grail" is used for a vessel — a cup, perhaps — but this is only a picture, a symbolic picture. It was never said in any other form what this power called "Grail" is — it was understood that every individual had to find the reality of the Grail for himself. And those who had found it were called "Knights of the Grail." There were such people, such "Knights of the Grail," and they were of importance in the early Middle Ages, in the lawless, Dark Ages. It was said — the Knights of King Arthur fight the brutish robbers and keep them in check by the power of the sword. But the Knights of the Grail go amongst the evil people and prevail on them to change, to become good men. They do this by the power of their words. The Knights of Arthur are the knights of the sword — the Grail Knights are the knights of the word.

But when the Albigensian Crusade destroyed all these traditions, there were two ways in which they were saved and preserved. One way was through the troubadours — Wolfram, Chrétien de Troyes and others. And there was still another way.

The stories of the troubadours reached only the ruling classes, the nobles and knights. For the peasants, the villains and serfs, the work of the troubadours was as remote as the moon — but they, too, were fond of stories, and what they enjoyed were the fold tales, the fairy stories which are now only for young children. All the fairy stories — "Snow White," "Cinderella" — which are now only for children were, originally, tales going round amongst the peasant population. The famous Grimm's fairy tales were collected by two brothers called Grimm from amongst peasants who had passed them on for many generations.

And some of these fairy tales originated amongst the Albigenses. Let us take one which is perhaps the best known.

A man, passing a garden, saw a beautiful rose, and went in and picked the flower to bring to his daughter, called "Beauty." But the owner of the garden was a hideous Beast. The Beast caught the man plucking the flower, and he could only save his life by promising the Beast to send him his daughter, Beauty. So Beauty was sent to the Beast, and though she was surrounded by servants and given beautiful rooms to live in, she was unhappy, and she refused the Beast's wish that she should marry him.

And one day, the wish to be free from this horrible creature from whom she could not escape became so strong that she wished he were dead. With this wish in her mind, she went into the garden, and saw, to her shock, the Beast lying motionless on the ground. At the sight, she felt shame for her wish, and pity for the poor, ugly creature. She ran to a fountain, and brought water and tried to revive him. The Beast opened his eyes, and said: "You wish me dead — and, as you will not marry me, I want to die." And then Beauty, moved by compassion, said: "No, you shall not die — I agree to marry you." And in this moment, the hideous beast changed — it became a handsome young prince. Her words had broken the evil spell of a magician who had turned him into an ugly beast until a beautiful girl would, by her free will, agree to marry him.

This story and all the others which tell of frogs, or bears, which are really princes, and freed from their enchantment by a girl willing to accept their companionship are all tales of Manichean origin — they are tales to make us aware that the dark forces of the subconscious can be transformed into powers of good. Fairy tales, too, have a meaning, and are, in fact, often quoted in modern books on psychology.

Parsifal Joins
King Arthur's Knights

Parsifal searched in vain for the lake where he had first seen the
Fisher King, for the Castle Montsalvage on the forest-clad hill.
He searched in vain, but he would not give up. His cousin
Sigune had called him "accursed" because he had failed to ask a
question that was expected of him. And from what she said, it
seemed that this question would have restored the health of the
ailing Fisher King, and it would have brought great honour to
Parsifal himself. And although he longed to return to his wife,
Queen Condwiramur, he could not go back until he had dis-
charged this debt, until he found the Grail and its guardian
knights and had asked the question. And so, whilst every wish in
him drew him back to the city of Belrepeire and its beautiful
queen, he did not return but continued his search.

Weeks passed, and months — the seasons changed, winter
came, and Parsifal rode through a landscape blanketed in snow,
still on his quest for Montsalvage, the castle of the Grail.

He did not know it, but he had come near a camp of King
Arthur and his knights. They had put up tents near a forest
where they intended to enjoy a sport greatly favoured by all
knights — the sport of falconry. For this sport, the hunters rode
out with falcons perched on their gauntlets. The falcon's heads
were covered with a hood. When the hunters saw a flight of wild
geese, they took the hoods off the falcons and threw them into
the air. The birds took wing, pounced on some of the wild geese
and brought them down. Then they had to be lured back by
scraps of food, to be caught again.

Such a hunt had been on just a day before Parsifal passed this
way. But one of Arthur's falcons had not come back — it had

stayed all night in the woods. And just as Parsifal came riding by, a flight of wild geese rose in the cold morning air, and the falcon winged after them and struck one goose with its claws. But the goose escaped with a wound on its neck, and from this wound three drops of blood fell on the snow, right in front of Parsifal.

As his eyes fell on the pink patches in the white snow, Parsifal reined his horse in. By some strange accident, the pink and white before him seemed to form a face, the face of Condwiramur. Perhaps no-one else would have seen any resemblance between the patches and a human face, but for Parsifal — who could not help thinking of her on his lonely quest — for Parsifal it was as if the hand of a master painter had created a living likeness of her in the snow.

He could not take his eyes from the image in the snow — he lost all sense of place and time, and was completely lost in thought about Condwiramur.

A squire had been sent out to look for the lost falcon. He saw a knight in red armour, staring down from his horse at the snow, and he asked the knight politely if he had seen a trained falcon. But the red knight took not the slightest notice of him — the squire was annoyed at this rudeness, and returned to the camp with bitter complaints about a strange knight who showed no respect for a servant of King Arthur. This was an insult that could not be allowed to pass. Immediately, one of King Arthur's knights rode out into the forest to teach the stranger better manners. He approached the stationary horseman, and shouted a challenge at him. But Parsifal was completely lost in thought, and did not even hear that someone shouted at him. He remained as still as a statue. The other knight was not used to being treated as if he were nothing. He lowered his spear, and galloped towards Parsifal. But, at the last moment, some kind of sixth sense warned Parsifal and roused him — he turned his horse, lowered his spear, and with one mighty thrust he threw the attacker from the saddle. He then turned again to the contemplation of the pink patch in the snow, forgetting everything else around him.

The knight of King Arthur had fallen on his arm and broken it, so he could not continue the argument in a knightly fashion.

He limped back to the camp and made it known how ill he had fared at the hands of this rude stranger.

There was keen competition amongst the knights for the privilege of teaching this ruffian courtly manners. In the end, it was Sir Kay whom King Arthur appointed to deal with the stranger. Sir Kay was the knight who had insulted Parsifal when he came to the court, and who had struck the lady whose laughter had proclaimed Parsifal the best of all knights.

Sir Kay rode into the forest until he saw the stranger, gazing at the snow before him. He rode close to him and shouted at him: "Get ready to fight, you lout!" And when the stranger continued to stare at the snow without moving, Sir Kay took his spear and gave that silent figure such a clout on the helmet that the whole forest rang.

This did the trick — it woke Parsifal promptly, but too promptly for Sir Kay, for the next moment he received a spear-thrust against his shield which sent him flying through the air and crashing down so heavily that he broke his right arm and left leg.

Then Parsifal returned again to the daydreams over his snow patch, whilst Sir Kay managed to climb on to his horse and returned to the camp with a tale of woe.

But now one of King Arthur's best knights, Sir Gawain, undertook to save the honour of the Round Table. Gawain had listened to the tales about the odd behaviour of the stranger, and it seemed to him that this was not the action of someone who was deliberately insulting King Arthur and his knights. This was not a man spoiling for a fight — perhaps the riddle of this stranger could be solved in a different manner.

And so, to everybody's surprise, Gawain rode into the forest unarmed, without spear or shield. And, like the others before him, Gawain saw the strange knight looking down on the snow before him, lost to the world and motionless. And, like the others before him, Gawain spoke to the stranger — he pleaded with him, he reproached him for lack of courtesy, for insulting King Arthur, and he promised him that if he would now come peacefully to the king he would be forgiven and made welcome.

But this well-mannered approach had as little effect as had the challenge of the others before Gawain. It brought no reply, no response from the stranger — he kept on staring at the snow. Now Gawain himself looked at the snow patch which held the stranger's attention, and thought he could discern the outline of a woman's face in the pink of snow and blood. "Well!" he said to himself. "A man in love! There's no accounting what such men will do. But there is only one way to bring this fellow to his senses." And Gawain dismounted, and took a scarf he wore, and spread it over the pink patch in the snow.

And it worked. Parsifal looked up, looked around him like a man waking from a dream. He was surprised to see the snow around him trampled by many horses' hooves. He was surprised to see that the point of his spear was broken — and who was the unarmed knight before him?

It took some time until he could take in what Gawain told him — that he had fought two knights and made them invalids. But he was very pleased to hear that one of the two invalids was Sir Kay. He had once promised that he would punish Sir Kay for striking a lady — and now this old account was settled. And as Sir Kay had been punished, there was no longer any reason which could keep him from King Arthur's court, and he gladly accepted Gawain's invitation.

And so Parsifal came to King Arthur, and was given a warm welcome. The lad who had once ridden his horse into the banqueting hall, who had come in fool's dress and knew nothing of chivalry, now returned as a knight of fame, who had rescued Queen Condwiramur and gained himself a crown.

And this knightly deed had earned him an honour coveted by every Christian knight — he was invited by King Arthur to join the companionship of the Round Table, to become a Knight of the Round Table. A banquet was given to celebrate the occasion, and it was a great moment in Parsifal's life when he took his seat at the Round Table, as the equal and companion of the most valiant knights in Christendom. This was the moment when the great dream which had lured him from the forest came true.

But this day, which might have been a day of supreme happiness for Parsifal, was also the day on which a cruel blow of fate destroyed his happiness.

They were all still sitting at the banquet and the whole company was in gay and happy mood, when a visitor arrived, at whose sight they all fell silent. The gay laughter ceased, and awe and fear descended like a cloud upon the company. The strange visitor was a woman, richly dressed in silk and brocade. Jewels gleamed on her headband, and on her dress — but all the rich ornaments could do little to improve this woman's looks. Her long sharp nose was like the beak of a hawk, her skin was sallow, and beneath bushy eyebrows a pair of piercing black eyes looked grimly at the company.

As she stared at them in silence, Parsifal heard the knights beside him whisper, "That's Cundry — Cundry, the messenger of the Grail, the servant of the Fisher King — her coming bodes evil for someone!" And when Parsifal heard these words, a great dread gripped his heart.

Cundry, the grim-faced woman, approached King Arthur, and said: "King of the Britons, you have brought shame upon yourself and upon all who serve you. You have allowed a man without honour, a man accursed, to take his place amongst you."

"It can't be true!" answered the King. "The Knights of the Round Table are all men of high honour. Who is the one you accuse of being unworthy?"

And the woman pointed with a long bony finger at Parsifal, and cried:"There is no honour amongst you, as long as he is in your midst!"

A gasp went through the whole great company of lords and ladies, and all eyes turned on Parsifal. And now the grim messenger spoke to him, "You may think that I am ugly, but although God has favoured you with good looks, you are a hundred times more repulsive than I am, for your heart and soul are rotten. You saw the suffering of the king whom I serve, but you did not find it in your heart to ask him what ailed him. You saw the wonders of the Grail, and your dull mind had no question. If you, unworthy son of a noble knight, had but asked once, my master would have blessed you, and your reward would have been higher than any you can dream of. But, as you have stayed dumb, the servants of the Grail must remain in grief — and you, blind fool, you are cursed!"

And before Parsifal could utter a word, Cundry strode out, and no-one knew where she went.

Shattered as he was, Parsifal could find comfort in the many knights and ladies who surrounded him and who assured him of their friendship, their love, their sympathy. But all those new-found and loyal friends could not shake him from the decision he had made when Cundry's accusation was shouted at him. He said: "As long as the curse is on me, I cannot belong to this noble company. As long as the curse is on me, I cannot return to the woman I love. I cannot find joy in life again, and I cannot rest until I have found Montsalvage again, and the suffering king, and have asked the question. I cannot rest, and I shall not rest, until I have found the Grail!"

The lords, the ladies, King Arthur himself, tried to persuade him to stay, in spite of Cundry's curse, but he would not listen to them. He knew that all the honours of the court would leave a bitter taste if he could not redeem the curse laid on him, if he could not make up for his omission.

And so the next day saw Parsifal setting out into the bleak winter weather on a search which might be endless, for he knew that only those whom the Grail called could find it. And now it was not the Grail which called him, only his own desire. The future that lay before him as he rode away was as bleak and grey as the wintry sky above him.

So it was that when Parsifal reached his fondest dream, his highest ambition — to become a knight of King Arthur — this fulfilment became at the same time hollow and meaningless. He had to seek for something else, in loneliness, and not knowing if he would ever find it.

It is often so in life — to reach the goal of one's ambition means often only to find it is but an empty shell and that one's true aim is something quite different.

The Quest of the Question

If there is one thing in the Parsifal story which goes "against the grain," and which offends our sense of justice, it is the curse, the punishment laid on him for no good reason at all. It offends our sense of justice that he is punished for such a small matter: not asking a question. And what makes it worse is that he did not even know that this question was expected of him. And he only refrained from asking that question because he followed the rules he had been taught by that old knight, Gurnemant.

It is an absurdity — it does not make sense. But do you think that the poet who wrote the story, Wolfram, was not aware of it? For the people of his own time, the rank injustice of it all was even more upsetting than it is for us — and if Wolfram put such a story before them, then he did it intentionally.

It was as if he would say: take the whole thing superficially, and it will seem an absurdity — you must go deeper to understand what I am driving at.

Now take that terrible thing Parsifal is said to have done: he has not asked a question. Wolfram goes out of his way to emphasise that the whole guilt of Parsifal consists just in this: he has not asked a question. Are questions all that important? Well, in our time, in the present age, they are.

All science begins with questions — why? how? where does this come from? Science is nothing else but a continuous process of asking questions. And as soon as an answer is found, it leads on to new questions. Every experiment in the laboratory is a question, every rocket sent into space is a question. All technical progress of our time has come from questions.

But it is not only the scientist who occupies himself with questions. Not everybody can be a scientist. But think of the millions who read and enjoy a detective story. And the pleasure of a detective story is that you live for a time with the question: "Who dunnit?" Or think of the popular panel games on television, the question and answer games. Think of all the people who spend hours on crossword puzzles. Or think of modern art — every modern painting is an experiment, and a puzzle, and people buy these paintings because they like to be puzzled — which means to have a question.

We question everything — the relationship between parents and children, the relations between the sexes, religion, government, standards of behaviour — these all give rise to questions.

It has to be like that, for it is in the nature of our time to ask questions. We won't take anything for granted — we ask and ask again. Our time is the age of questions.

But it was not so in the past. In past ages, people were not so curious, they did not ask so many questions. Nor did the Church encourage questions. The few who began to ask questions were called "heretics" and burnt at the stake.

But there was already in those dark ages something else ... it was a kind of preparation for the coming age, for the future. The ceaseless seeking and searching and questioning of our time had a kind of preparation — a first dim beginning. You see, a knight of that time did not always stay in his castle or in the court of his king. From time to time, the knight set out on a journey in search of a difficult and dangerous task. And such a seeking for a great, worthy task was called a "quest." And all the story books of that time, all the stories told by the troubadours, glorified the quests of knights, the quests of Lancelot or Guinevere.

But the word "quest" means the same as the word "question" — it means a seeking, a searching.

The knights were not yet ready to seek and search with their minds — they did not ask questions: they had to do their seeking and searching physically, by going on a quest. Their quests were the beginning, the preparation for the age of questions in which we live nowadays.

The other poets in Wolfram's time wrote stories about such "quests" — but Wolfram was different. He was himself a "heretic," who dared to ask questions forbidden by the Church.

And his hero was to be a hero of the future, a hero of the time when all men would ask questions as Wolfram did.

And that is why Parsifal is from the beginning shown to be full of questions. He was to be a hero of questions — full of curiosity.

But Wolfram, the poet, wanted also to show that there were enemies who did not want this new force of questioning coming into the world. There was the Roman Church — but, you know, the Church would not have held such power if there had not been a majority of people who were against anything new, against any curiosity: they all wanted things to go on for ever in the same way. They were the people who supported the Church and held it in power.

And Wolfram described such a person in the old man, Gurnemant, who became the teacher of Parsifal. Gurnemant is not an evil person — he has the best intentions — but he is too old, too wrapped up in old conventions and rules to understand the new thing that is in Parsifal. And that is why this old man, Gurnemant, stops Parsifal's flow of questions, by telling him: "It's bad manners, it's wrong to ask questions."

In this meeting between the old man and the young man, the poet gave a picture of the meeting between the past and the future. And the past, with the authority of age and experience, imposes on the young man the dead conventions and rules which have been observed for centuries. The ignorant young man, Parsifal, can do nothing else, but accepts these rules, and all his curiosity, all the questions which are natural to him, are stifled — they are buried under the conventions he learns from the old man.

And when, later, Parsifal comes to the Fisher King, he does not act out of his own true nature, he is not true to himself, but follows a rule which is, really, foreign to him — he does not ask any questions.

That is a great pity, but it is not something you could blame Parsifal for. It is not a crime — but if nothing else happened Parsifal would live to the end of his life not according to his own true nature, but according to conventions which are foreign and unnatural to him. He would not be a free human being — for to be free means to act from one's own inner being — he would be a slave of conventions. And to live like that is a curse. That is what the story means by the "curse" on Parsifal. To be unfree, to be a slave of conventions — that is a curse.

Parsifal has to be rescued from this fate: to become a conventional good knight, he must be rescued, and his own true nature, and the thirst for questions, must be reawakened in him. He needs a hard shaking to bring to light in him what is buried under the conventions — and that is what happens to him.

So, you see, what happens to Parsifal seems to be a punishment, a grossly unfair punishment — but it is really a kind of painful education, a re-education, to bring out his true nature. Parsifal has lost his true self — he has to find himself again, and all the unhappiness now inflicted on him is for the purpose of making him what he really is: a man of the future, a man who asks questions.

In a school, it can happen that pupils who makes poor progress are put in a lower class — this is not done to punish them, it is done to give them a better chance. Well, Parsifal, by his strange upbringing and nature, belonged to an older class — he belonged to the future, to the age of questions. But this true nature of Parsifal had been stifled, and so he had to go into a lower class, he had to go back to something which was a preparation for the future — he had to go on a quest. In history, humankind had to go on quests before it could reach the age of questions. And so Parsifal has to go on a quest until the power of questions has grown in him again.

And that is why he is sent on a quest — the quest of the holy Grail. He searches for the holy Grail. This is his quest — but it is not a punishment, it is a rescue, a help and an education. He did not ask the question — so he must go on a quest, the quest of the holy Grail.

Wolfram, the poet, could not say openly what he meant — not in the time in which he lived. He could only put it cautiously into pictures — but by making the story of Parsifal's punishment so absurd, he really put up a signpost: "Please don't take this superficially — there is a deeper meaning behind it."

But this part of the story also has a very realistic meaning for

our own time. Science has become what it is — the greatest
force in modern life — only by asking questions. But as science
grew and developed, there also came men who were regarded as
authorities. Unfortunately, these "authorities of science"
became, and still are, just as narrow-minded and dogmatic as the
medieval Church — they suppress new questions and persecute
"heretics."

Not so long ago, a biologist submitted to the British Medical
Association a report on a remarkable discovery he had made, a
discovery which could save countless lives and shorten many ill-
nesses. The wise men of the British Medical Association shook
their heads. It was quite impossible — and no doctor worthy of
that name would make use of this discovery. And when the biologist, in spite of this judgement of top scientists, carried on with
his research, he was shunned, scorned and condemned by the
whole profession. It took him fifteen years to break through this
wall of prejudice and convention — and then his discovery was
hailed as one of the great advances in medicine. The name of the
discovery was penicillin, and the scientist who discovered it was
Alexander Fleming. Fleming refused to take a patent on his discovery — he gave it to the world without making any profit for
himself. This was the man whom the "authorities" had scorned
and treated as a fool.

These authorities were just like old Gurnemanz. No-one
had asked before Fleming: "Can a fungus kill bacteria?" And
when asked that question, he was told it was wrong to ask such a
question.

That is the danger — that the scientists themselves forget
that questions are the lifeblood of science, and that no-one has
the right to say that this question is allowed, and that question is
not allowed. Once I spoke to a very intelligent scientist about
such questions as: "Is there life after death?" And he said, with
enormous authority,: "This is not a question that concerns science — this is not a scientific question. Believe it, or don't
believe it, but leave science out of it!" I could only answer:
"What is your authority to say so? Perhaps your own corner of
science has nothing to say to this question. But what right have
you to set limits to science as a whole? How can you know that

a science for such questions is not possible? You talk like the medieval Church, or like the old man, Gurnemanz, in the story of Parsifal."

So, when you go out into the world, don't let the Gurnemanzes in the world, clever as they are, tell you what questions are scientific or permissible. No-one has the right to stifle the questions you want to ask. Remember Parsifal, who nearly lost himself by accepting some outworn conventions.

The Grail

Parsifal had sworn to himself that he would neither return to his wife nor resume his place amongst the knights of the Round Table until he had found the castle of the Grail — until the quest of the holy Grail was accomplished. But when he made this promise, he had little idea of what kind of task he had set himself.

He travelled through many lands, and his life was in constant danger. Armed knights challenged him, and barred his way. Robbers and bandits waylaid him for the sake of riches they expected to find on him. On other occasions he had to come to the rescue of the weak and oppressed against their persecutors. But it was as if he had a charmed life, because in all those encounters he overcame his opponents, or drove them to flight. A charmed life — but to Parsifal it was a life empty and hollow unless he could find the castle of the Grail. He found no thrill in the dangers, and no satisfaction in his victories.

There were times when he found himself far from any village or castle, and he rode through bare lands in utter loneliness. On such lonely nights, he saw sometimes the moon as a crescent in the sky — and the gleaming arc above him reminded him of the shining vessel he had seen in the Fisher King's hall: it reminded him of the Grail, and filled his heart with indescribable longing.

But the silvery crescent in the sky enclosed only darkness — there was only darkness between its horns, and it seemed to Parsifal like a picture of himself. He felt he was himself such an empty vessel, such an empty shell — and this void in him could only be filled if he could find the goal of his quest.

At times, he had experiences between sleeping and waking, dreamlike visions which filled him with dread. He saw in such a vision a little chapel on a roadside. And, in this dream, he entered the chapel and saw, lying on the altar, a dead knight. A candle burnt with a steady flame in front of the dead man. And, as Parsifal in this dream vision stared at the strange sight, a vast black arm appeared and its black hand reached for the candle and extinguished it ... and all was darkness.

Beset by dangers outside, harassed by this feeling of emptiness in himself, disturbed by such visions, Parsifal yet continued with his search. But, as time passed, his heart became filled with bitterness and resentment. What had he done to deserve such a fate? It was easy for people who enjoyed happy and contented living to believe in a kind, loving God. But it had not been a kind, loving God for Parsifal. He felt no reason to feel grateful to such a god — and he began to look with scorn at the people he saw on Sundays or feast-days going to church. Let them believe that their prayers meant anything — but he himself would have nothing to do with this kind of thing!

Yet, in spite of the bitterness and hardness and despair he felt, he continued with his search — he continued on his quest — out of stubbornness, out of a grim determination not to abandon a task he had set himself.

It was already the fifth year of the quest — for five years he had travelled far and wide, and searched in vain. Now it was early spring again, but Parsifal had no eyes for the buds on the trees, for the fresh green in the fields. Nor did he notice that several knights he met on the road wore neither armour nor weapons, and were dressed in white. He did not notice the strange looks they gave him, nor did he hear when one of them shouted after him: "Don't you know what day it is?"

Immersed in his own unhappy thoughts, and oblivious of the world around him, he rode on, and followed the road which took him into a forest. And, deep in the forest, Parsifal came upon a hut, a hermit's hut.

A hermit was a man who withdrew from life in the world, who withdrew to the solitude of a forest or a mountain, to devote himself entirely to a life of prayer and meditation.

Parsifal, in the mood he was in, would have passed the hermit's hut without giving it a thought. But the hermit himself came out and hailed him. "Sir Knight," said the hermit. "What has come upon you that you ride out in armour, with spear and sword, on this day of all days?"

Parsifal looked at the hermit — a man whose hair and beard were white with age. To old people, courtesy was due, and so he answered the question, and said:"I have learned to be ready for a fight at any time. Why should I not be ready for danger on this day?"

The hermit shook his head and said: "Perhaps you are not a Christian. Perhaps you are a Muslim and then, of course, you don't know what this day is. But amongst Christian folk this is a day on which no battle is fought, on which no tournament takes place, a day on which no sword must be drawn — no knight will put on his armour, or carry weapons. Today, Sir Knight, is Good Friday, the day on which Christ died on the cross. On this day, in remembrance of Him who gave his life but would not allow Peter to defend him with a sword — on this day, no Christian will engage in fight or harm another man. Are you not a Christian?"

Parsifal answered: "I remember the rule now — one of the many I was taught once, and they brought me little happiness. But whether I am still a Christian, I don't know. I have not entered a church nor offered a prayer to God for many a year — and I would be a liar if I did. I do not even want to think of God — for all he has given me is a fruitless search and grief and sorrow. He has forgotten me — and I have forgotten Him."

The hermit sighed, and then said: "This is but foolish speech, Sir Knight — there may well come the day when you will give thanks to God for the very thing that is now your complaint. Come, dismount — take off the armour and let me be your host on this holy day. And perhaps you can tell me what has made you so sore at God and the world."

Parsifal hesitated — what use was it to tell this old man of his troubles? But then he felt that it would be a relief to unburden himself to a sympathetic listener. And soon, divested of armour and weapons, he told the hermit that he had now been for may years on a fruitless quest, a quest for the Grail.

"A quest for the Grail," said the hermit. "Don't you know

that no-one can find the Grail unless the Grail itself calls him? I know it — for I have been myself a knight of the Grail before I became a hermit."

"You have been a knight of the Grail?" cried Parsifal, astonished.

"Yes," answered the hermit, "and, as you are a seeker for the Grail, I will tell you the story. At the time of Christ, there lived amongst the Jews a pious man, and a follower of Christ. His name was Joseph of Arimathea. And when Jesus Christ celebrated the Last Supper with his disciples, it was in the house of this man Joseph. And the cup which Jesus and the disciples used to drink the wine of the Last Supper remained with Joseph, and he guarded it as a holy relic — for it has power such as no other vessel has. And there was also another holy thing that remained in the keeping of Joseph — it was the spear that pierced the side of Christ when he was on the cross.

"In secret, the cup and the spear were passed from generation to generation, and only their guardians knew where they were. And in time the cup and the spear came into the keeping of a noble knight, a man without fault and without vice. And he was told in a dream vision to build a castle to house the cup and the spear, and that the best knights would be called to serve and guard the holy things.

"The cup is called 'Grail,' and every year on Good Friday a white dove appears and places a wafer in the Grail. And this gives the Grail its powers, for he who sees the Grail needs no other nourishment — he is nourished by seeing it. And he who is ill needs no other cure — he is healed by the sight of the Grail.

"Yet — there is one man who is ill and suffering, and has to see the Grail: but the sight does not cure him, and does not help him, and he must bear the pain until a strange and dark prophecy is fulfilled."

"Who is this man? Why must he suffer? What is the prophecy?" cried Parsifal, who realized that all this concerned him deeply.

And the hermit answered: "He is the King of the Grail — they also call him the Fisher King — and his name is Anfortas. It was his father who built the Castle Montsalvage that houses the

Grail, and who was the king and leader of the first knights of the Grail. When the father became old and infirm, there appeared on the Grail in shining letters the name 'Anfortas,' and that meant that Anfortas should become Lord of the Grail. And Anfortas was a valiant knight, and did great deeds in the service of the Grail But no servant of the Grail must seek adventure and battle to gain glory and honour for himself. Only selfless deeds can be done by the knights of the Grail. And Anfortas sinned against this rule, and for a woman's sake, to gain glory and favour in her eyes, he went and made war. It was in these fights that he received the wound, and no herb or ointment in the world can heal it — nor does the Grail heal it. That is his punishment for having failed, as King of the Grail, to remain free of vanity and selfishness."

"But when he was brought back to the castle, there appeared writing on the Grail. It said:
Wait for the day when he comes who
Will ask, "O King, what ails you?"
And when he asks, the wound will heal.
Yet no-one must to him reveal
That he should ask. Out of his own
Compassion he must ask, alone.
And since then Anfortas has been in never-ending pain, hoping and living for the day when the deliverer should come. But I myself left the service of the Grail to pray for him — to pray that God may hasten the day of his deliverance. For, you see, I am his brother, Trevricent. I gave up the privilege of seeing the Grail, the honour of being its keeper, in the hope that my sacrifice would be accepted by God and shorten my brother's agony.

"Since then, I heard that a knight did come — but, alas, the fool did not ask ... he asked no question at all, and so he earned shame and not honour."

The hermit fell silent — and Parsifal too sat in silence. Should he tell Trevricent, the hermit, who he was? But he had never lacked courage, and so he said to the old man: "I was that knight — I kept silent at the sight of the Grail, and at the sight of the suffering king. I am Parsifal, the son of Herzeloyde — I was brought up in the forest, and when I left the forest and learned the rules of courtesy I was foolish enough to let them prevent me from asking the question."

At these words, Trevricent took the young man's hand in his own, and said: "Whatever you have done, I am glad to see you, Parsifal, for you are my sister's son. Queen Herzeloyde was my sister — and the sister of the poor King Anfortas. The blood of the Kings of the Grail is in you, Parsifal, and that is why you found the Grail's castle!"

"Yes," said Parsifal, with bitterness, "and that privilege given to me by my blood — I have lost it, and now I cannot find the Grail, and have spent years in a fruitless quest."

"No," said the hermit. "I feel it is no accident that has brought you here on Good Friday. The Providence that has brought you to me will also guide you at the right time to the Grail, and to the deliverance of your uncle, the Lord of the Grail. And when that time comes, you will, perhaps, also understand that your long search and what you suffered was not in vain."

And for the first time in many years there was again hope in Parsifal's heart, and a feeling that there was a higher wisdom in human destiny.

He was a different man when, some days later, after Easter, he left Trevricent to continue his quest for the Grail.

Darkness and the God of Freedom

Wolfram describes in his story how Parsifal, embittered by his fruitless search, turns against God. In the whole literature of the Middle Ages, this is the first time that somebody says:"I can do without God — I can do without religion."

The Middle Ages were the "Age of Faith" — and the time in which men left their homes and families to go on a crusade, to fight and die for their religion. There were "heretics," but the heretics also died and suffered willingly for their beliefs — there were Jews and Muslims equally ardent in their religion. But there were no men who would say: "I do not need a belief in God — I do not need any religion at all."

And when Parsifal in his bitterness quite openly defies all the religions, when he refuses to take part in any prayer or worship, when he shows that he can live without religion, then he does not speak as a man of the Middle Ages — he speaks with the voice of modern man.

By some kind of intuition, by some kind of prophetic foresight, the poet, Wolfram, realized that his hero, Parsifal, the hero of the future, must also come to the point where he rejects God, denies God and lives without religion. In his prophetic vision, Wolfram realized that in the future men would come to the point where they turned away from religion — and so his hero Parsifal must come to the same point, and so speak as no man of the age of chivalry, the age of faith, would have spoken.

Parsifal wears the dress and armour of a medieval knight — but he is a modern man even in his rejection of God and religion.

The time which, for the poet, Wolfram, was a distant future, that time has now arrived — it is our present time. There is not just one single Parsifal saying: "I can live without religion, without God" — there are millions. If the Middle Ages were the age of faith, the age of belief, then our time is the age of unbelief, the age of atheism.

There are millions today who say: "I can only believe in something I can see or touch — and I won't believe in something like 'God' or 'spirit' which can't be seen or touched." You might think that this is the result of the progress of science — you might think that science has taught us to trust only our senses. But it is not so at all.

What science has shown us is that we cannot trust our senses at all. There are the infrared and ultraviolet rays of the sunlight, which our eyes cannot see at all — but they exist, and are real just the same. There is magnetism: a piece of magnetic iron looks and feels just the same as a piece of ordinary iron. We have no sense organ for magnetic forces — but magnetism exists, and is real, just the same. There are electromagnetic waves and radiations pouring in from the cosmos, from space, which we are just beginning to investigate — there are forces which, a few decades ago, one could not even guess at, but our senses can tell us nothing about them.

The lesson of science is that our senses, our eyes and ears, are not fit to judge what exists and what does not exist, what is real and what is not real.

What are the forces used in hypnosis? We have no instrument to measure the forces which produce hypnosis, we have no sense organ to show us what they look like, but they work, they are real, just the same.

And so, when people say: "I don't believe in God, I don't believe in a spiritual world, because I can't see them," it is not because of science, but for a very different reason. The reason why people become atheists, materialists, these reasons are not in the world around us, not in the science which explores this world, but in the human soul, in the human mind.

One of the most common and most silly prejudices is the assumption that the human mind remains always the same. We assume that, perhaps, a caveman or a knight of the Middle Ages was not quite so clever as we are — he did not know as much as we know today — but otherwise the human mind was always the same, and worked in the same way. But this very common and very silly assumption is not at all borne out by facts. One has to read the works of anthropologists, and the works of historians who study the mentality of the past, to come to the true picture. And the true picture shows enormous changes, even over a few centuries.

Take the Middle Ages — the Age of Faith. If you read and study any books written in the eleventh, twelfth, thirteenth centuries, then you realize that certain words had a different meaning, and even a different effect, in those days from what they have today.

When a man of the Middle Ages used or heard a word like "God" or "Jesus," these words filled the soul with a warm, living glow, with an inner radiance. Just as, for us, the word "death" rouses automatically a certain feeling of dread — or, to take a very concrete example, the words "lemon juice" can bring the taste of lemon juice to your tongue — so for a man of the Middle Ages words like "God" or "Christ" had a certain effect, a warm inner glow — a feeling of comfort and security.

Young children, who are a bit like human beings of the past, still often have such a feeling — this feeling of warmth and comfort when they hear or speak the name of God.

In the Middle Ages this feeling was common, it was natural, and this is why the Middle Ages were the "Age of Faith" — because the words "God" and "Christ" still had this effect, a kind of warmth and comfort.

But, if you go then to later centuries and read books, even religious books, written by devout, pious people, you can see — it is quite obvious — that the words no longer have the same effect. The warmth, the glow, has become less and less.

And in our time, the glow has gone. The words "God" or "spirit" have become like empty shells. For a small number of people, there is still a little glow in these words — and they are the few sincerely religious people who still exist today.

But for the great majority of present-day humanity, these words have no longer any effect, or any meaning. Some are afraid of admitting it — they pretend that there is something in the words — and they are the people who cling to some religious practice, as a custom, as a habit, but it is a pretence.

A great number of people, however, cannot see any point in pretending — they cannot see any point in putting up a show, they are content to live without religion, and without God.

These are the three possibilities — the few who can still feel something in the word "God" and so find satisfaction in their religion; those who cannot feel anything, but pretend they can; and those for whom the words "God," "Christ," "Spirit" have no meaning, and who say so and live without religion.

But there is still another alternative. There are people for whom the word "God" has no longer any meaning — it is as if there is an emptiness, a vacant place in the soul where there used to be a radiance, a glow. But these people feel the necessity to seek for a new meaning of the words "God," "Christ," "Spirit."

The old meaning, the old light and glow, have gone from the words — there is only emptiness and darkness left — but there is perhaps a new meaning to be found, somehow, somewhere.

It might be a long search to find the new meaning — it may be a fruitless search, it may be a search in the wrong places, it may be a search for something which cannot be found. But there are people who search for this new meaning — and this is the modern search for the holy Grail.

So, as a person of this present age, you have really four alternatives. You either still feel some reality in the name of God, and so can pray and worship in sincerity. Or you do not feel anything, but find it to your advantage to make a show of religion. Or you do not pretend, and do without religion.

Or you become a seeker, a person in search of a new meaning of the words, a modern Parsifal in search of the Grail.

These are the four roads before you, and every person in our time has to take one of these four roads. But whatever road you take, it is your own choice.

No-one else can take the decision for you — no-one else has the power to make you go on one road or the other. It is your own personal decision.

But it was not like that in the past. In the past, when the names of "God" or "Christ" still had, one could say, an almost magical power, this was not anybody's personal choice. It was a kind of instinct. You know that there are kinds of birds which migrate; when autumn comes, they fly to a warmer climate, to the south, to Africa. They do not fly from choice, they do not fly south because they have, each one, decided that this is the best thing to do when winter comes. A swallow does not have to think and to decide about it — the force of instinct compels the swallow to fly south, and the force of instinct guides it to Africa.

And, as far as religion is concerned, a man of the Middle Ages was no more his own master than the swallow is. As the swallow inherits the instinct which drives it south, so the man of the Middle Ages inherited the instinct which made him feel warmth and comfort in the name of God. It was in his blood — it was something inherited from his fathers.

It was only natural for these people to say "God of my fathers" — it was a correct description, because the feeling for God was an inherited instinct, something in the blood, inherited from their fathers and forefathers.

But this instinct died, just as many other instincts which men used to have died in the course of history. The instinct that was inherited, that was in the blood — that instinct died, and that is why the glow disappeared and the age of faith disappeared.

You think, perhaps, that people took up science from the fourteenth/fifteenth century onwards because they became suddenly clever — they became suddenly cleverer than the people who lived a few centuries earlier.

No — they took to science because the instinct which had guided and directed men as it guides and directs the swallows, this instinct had died out.

If the swallows lost their instinct, they would have to make maps and use a compass to find their way to Africa — they would have to explore and discover. It does not happen to the swallows, but it did happen to man. His instinct died and, bewildered in a strange world, he began to explore.

The man of the Middle Ages found certainty and comfort in God by an instinct, not out of any personal choice.

But in us, today, that instinct is dead. And whatever road we take, whichever of the four roads I have mentioned we choose, it is a personal choice — it is a free choice.

We are deprived of the guidance of instinct, we are left in the dark — but we have gained something: we have gained freedom, the freedom to choose the road on which we want to travel.

We could not say: "God of our fathers," as men used to say. We would have to say "God of Freedom," God who leaves us free to seek Him or to forget Him.

But the price of this freedom is that the instinct died, and that we are left in darkness.

And now think of that dream picture which Parsifal saw when he was on his fruitless quest and his soul turned away from religion.

In this dream picture he saw a chapel, which is a religious building. In the chapel there was the corpse of a knight. This dead knight is a symbolic picture of that dead instinct that used to guide men.

And there was a solitary burning candle, which is the last glow of that inner light, that inner glow men used to experience. And a black hand extinguishes the candle, and all is in darkness. This darkness is a picture of the soul once the guidance of instinct and the warm comforting glow of faith have gone.

The dream is really a picture of Parsifal's own soul — the dream describes in a picture what actually happens — that he turns away from religion. Darkness has come to Parsifal — as it has come for us.

And the only thing that remains to Parsifal is also what remains for us: that in the darkness, out of our own choice, out of freedom, we seek for a new meaning of God, that we seek for the Grail.

But in that darkness which makes us free in our choice, which leaves us free to seek the Grail or not to seek it, in that darkness something does take place, something happens to Parsifal on his lonely and seemingly hopeless quest.

Do you get the impression that Parsifal is enjoying this fruitless quest for the Grail? No — he suffers. He is sad, unhappy — a man weighed down by grief. And he does not like suffering —

no human being does. But do you think that a person who never suffered — if there is such a person — could feel pity or compassion for another human being? We can only sympathize, we can only feel for someone else's suffering because we have suffered ourselves.

Of course, we can always feel a bit sorry for somebody who is ill or in trouble, just because we have known at least a little suffering ourselves. But true, deep sympathy, a true compassion (which means literally to share the suffering of others) — true compassion is only born out of our own deep and real suffering.

The thick-skinned fellow whom nothing can hurt is not likely to take much notice of other people's distress.

Parsifal was thick-skinned enough to leave his mother without even noticing that she suffered. He was thick-skinned enough to kill the red knight and have no other thought but to get hold of his armour. There was very little compassion in Parsifal.

Imagine for a moment he had come to the Fisher King and had asked:"What is wrong with you?" He would have asked out of curiosity, but not out of compassion.

What he needed to learn was compassion, and the only way to learn it was through suffering himself. He had to suffer.

And that inner darkness, being deprived of religion, living without any feeling for God — that was part of the suffering.

Think of the Middle Ages, when people still had the instinct and felt warmth and comfort at the name of God. It was not a time of much pity and compassion. A saint like Francis of Assisi could feel compassion — he was a man who had imposed suffering on himself, by denying himself all the things that others lived for: wealth, honours, good food. But Francis was an exception. The other people of his time, with all their great faith and ardent religion, were pitiless to the point of cruelty.

And, in our time — godless, without religion as it is — there is far more compassion, a far greater feeling for the needs and suffering of other people. We have not only gained freedom, but compassion, since the old instincts died and disappeared.

And such a feeling as pity or compassion is something spiritual in the world. If the materialists, the atheists, are right — if there is no God, if there is neither soul nor spirit in man — then we would be no more than machines, complicated machines. Why should one machine feel for another machine? Machines do not feel — but we do. And any action performed out of pity, mercy, compassion, is proof of man's spiritual nature — and of God, who is pure compassion and love.

I have known people who were convinced atheists, materialists, but they were shining examples of true kindness and active compassion. But no matter how they denied God — in their feelings, in their actions they proved and asserted the spirit in man and the spirit of God.

In the darkness, where the old instinct lies dead, there grows the freedom of choice — and their grows compassion, the new instinct that leads to a new meaning of God: not the God of the fathers, but the God of freedom, the God of mercy and compassion, the God of love.

Parsifal had to live through the darkness, to seek God in freedom. He had to suffer — to learn compassion. And then he could, on a Good Friday, the day on which Christ suffered on the cross, meet the hermit who could give him new hope and an understanding that his suffering was necessary and would, in the end, lead to the Grail.

The Conclusion of the Quest

The poet Wolfram introduces at this stage of the story a new figure that may seem funny or nonsensical; but I think we know
already that Wolfram is not a poet who lets his fantasy roam
without reason, and that there is a meaning, a symbolic meaning
in his fantastic inventions. The new figure now brought into the
story is a very fantastic creature indeed — it is a man who is
black and white, like a magpie.

Moreover, having decided that he needs in his story such a
black and white person, Wolfram also wanted to make this
black-and-white man a brother — or at least a half-brother — of
Parsifal, and had to invent a story to make this possible.

So, when you hear this part of the story, keep in mind that,
odd or absurd as it sounds, the poet wants to convey something
— there is a meaning to it, a psychological meaning.

You remember that Parsifal was the son of Herzeloyde, who
brought him up in the forest, and of a king, Gamuret, who was
killed in battle when Parsifal was still a little child.

Now this father of Parsifal, Gamuret, was in his younger
days himself a knight who went on quests in search of adventure. And Gamuret, in his youth, roamed very far indeed — he
travelled to lands far from Europe, and came to a land where the
people were black. These"Moors" as they were called, were not
Christians, they were pagans. And these pagans were ruled by a
queen: she, too, was dark-skinned and a heathen, but very beautiful, and the young Gamuret fell in love with her. He fought for
her against her enemies and, in the end, he married her and a
son was born who was called Feirefiz. An in wolfram's sotry this
child, Feirefiz, the son of a white father and a black mother, was
black and white.

Within a year of the birth of this black-and-white son, his

mother, the queen, died. Gamuret, the father, left the child and the whole kingdom in the trust of the queen's brother, and set out again on further adventures. He returned to Europe, to Christian lands; he met Herzeloyde and married again. And, as we know, he was later killed in battle.

And so, while Parsifal grew up in the forest, there grew up in a far-away land his black-and-white half-brother, Feirefiz.

Feirefiz was brought up as a pagan by his uncle, and in time he became king of this land of Moors. But the blood of his father was strong in Feirefiz — he, too, loved adventure and knightly combat, and so he left his kingdom and went on a quest in search of danger and fights.

He was travelling one day through a forest when he saw, coming from the opposite direction, a knight in splendid red armour. This red knight was, of course, Parsifal.

For Feirefiz such a meeting could only have one purpose — a fight — and he called out immediately a challenge. And for Parsifal it was also a matter of course to accept the challenge.

And so they both lowered their spears and galloped against each other. But when the spears crashed on the shields, neither of them could unseat the other.

Both recognized that, for a combat with spears, they were too evenly matched. They threw the spears down and drew their swords. Parsifal used the sword he had once received from the Fisher King, the sword that would never break except in one danger — a danger only known to the sword's maker.

The two knights struck at each other with their swords, they hacked at each other's shields, they hit with such force that fiery sparks flew from helmet and armour — but even the most forceful blows brought no decision.

They had already been fighting for a whole hour — the forest was ringing with the clash of their weapons — they were both near the end of their great strength, when Parsifal summoned all the strength left to him, and struck a mighty blow at his opponent's helmet — and with this blow, his sword broke!

With the sword of the Fisher King broken, Parsifal was weaponless, and at the other man's mercy. But the other knight did not strike him down, he called out: "There is no honour in winning when the opponent cannot fight back! Let us call a truce and rest."

And so they dismounted, and stretched their tired limbs on the soft moss of the forest. They took off their helmets, and Parsifal was surprised to see the black-and-white face of the other knight. But the sight also brought back memories that his mother had once told him of his father's first marriage, and the strange black-and-white child born from that marriage.

He asked: "What is your name?"

And the other answered: "I am Feirefiz, the son of Gamuret."

"I, too, am a son of Gamuret," said Parsifal, "and now I know why my sword would not serve me, but broke — it would not serve me against my brother."

The two knights who had just fought each other so grimly now embraced each other, deeply moved that they had each found a brother. And when black-and-white Feirefiz heard of Parsifal's quest for the Holy Grail, he swore that he would not leave his new-found brother, but join him in the quest, no matter how long it would take.

So Parsifal was no longer alone in his quest — he now had a companion, his brother, Feirefiz.

And as the two now continued the journey, they had another meeting, which made Parsifal feel that his quest was no longer so hopeless as he had once thought.

They rode on through the forest and came upon a hut. Parsifal dismounted, and entered the hut — and in it he found his cousin, Sigune, with the coffin of her dead bridegroom.

But this time Sigune did not drive him away and call him "accursed," as she had once, on their last meeting. She looked aged and haggard — but she spoke in a mild voice, when she said: "Long has been your quest, Parsifal — and you have suffered, as I have suffered since death took the man who was to become my husband. Here on earth I could not become his wife — but I feel bound to him by my love, which death cannot end. And now I know that my grief will not last much longer. Soon my life will come to its end, and I shall be united with him who has gone from earth before me. But, as my own suffering will soon be ending, so will yours, Parsifal. Go in peace — we both shall find what we seek!"

There was not despair, but hope and joy in Sigune's voice, and when Parsifal left her, he felt a deep confidence filling his heart as he continued the journey with his brother.

And the next stage of this journey brought them to King Arthur and his knight. They came upon a large camp with men-at-arms and knights, for King Arthur had just ended a great war against a powerful enemy. Gawain, the loyal friend of Parsifal, had been the hero of this war, and it was Gawain who welcomed Parsifal and Feirefiz and presented them to King Arthur.

Although Parsifal had still not found the Grail, he could accept a day's hospitality from the King of Britain, and so he found himself sitting at table with the knights of King Arthur. And they all looked with wonder at his black-and-white brother.

And as they were sitting together, there came once again a visitor — a visitor whom they all recognized by the rich garments, by the jewels on headband and dress — it was Cundry, the messenger of the Grail.

And, once again, silence fell at her coming — and in every mind there was the question what ill, what curse, her coming might portend. But they all noticed that she wore now the Grail's coat of arms — the sign of a white dove.

Cundry gave a courteous greeting to King Arthur — then she approached Parsifal ... and fell to her knees before him. And when she looked up, her sharp and ugly features were transformed by an expression of great joy.

She said: "Parsifal, your quest is ended. The secrets of the Grail are written in the stars. As the planets move and change in their prescribed paths, they proclaim in heavenly writing the destiny of man here on earth. And the heavenly writing now speaks that your hour of destiny has come.

"You are called to the Grail, and you are called to the highest honour the Grail can give, for your name has appeared on the holy chalice. Your name, Parsifal — we saw it written as the name of the new King of the Grail.

"He who was king before, your uncle, Amfortas — the Fisher King — now waits for you to come and ask the question that will end his pain, and he will then serve you gladly and faithfully as his lord.

"And by the command written on the Grail, your wife, Condwiramur, has been brought to Montsalvage, to the castle of the Grail, to be at your side as queen. She, too, is now waiting for you there.

"We also saw it written that you are not to come alone. He of the black-and-white face, your brother Feirefiz, is to come with you to Montsalvage.

"And I, who once brought you ill tidings and sorrow, I am to lead you and your companion to that place which no-one can find unless he is called.

"So speaks the writing — so speak the stars — so speaks the Grail!"

What Parsifal felt at this message was not pride, it was not even joy, but a deep humility. The young lad, ambitious and eager, could feel pride and arrogance — but not the man who had suffered and had come to the end of his quest.

But once again Parsifal had to leave King Arthur and his knights — he was not meant to be one of them. But this leave-taking was not like the others before — this time he was leaving to receive the highest honour: the kingship of the Grail. And so the lady who had, by her laughter, prophesied the highest honour for him, had been right.

And so Parsifal saw again that lake where he had encountered the Fisher King without knowing he was his uncle. He saw again the winding, uphill path — but this time a band of knights came to meet him and his companions, and to form a guard of honour for the chosen one, the coming guardian of the Grail.

And when they entered the castle Montsalvage, there was no longer sadness on any face which welcomed them — there was joy and happiness.

Parsifal and Feirefiz were relieved of their armour and, dressed in white cloaks, they entered the great hall that had been in Parsifal's mind so often in the years of his quest.

And there, half sitting, half leaning on a couch, was the sufferer, Amfortas, the Fisher King. Parsifal embraced him, and said: "Uncle, I have failed you sadly the first time I came here, and so have made your pain last longer than it should have been. It means more than the kingship to me that I can now bring you relief and health. Amfortas — what is ailing you?"

And, at these words, the wound closed and healed, and strength and vigour returned — and the sick paleness of Amfortas changed to the glow of health. He rose from his couch — then he knelt down before Parsifal and said: "Son of my sister Herzeloyde — let me be the first to vow allegiance and faithful service to you as the chosen and worthy King of the Grail!"

Then a lady came forward, and it seemed to Parsifal that she was even more beautiful than the picture of her he had carried in his mind so many years — more beautiful than the picture he had once seen formed by blood and snow. They spoke few words, Condwiramur and Parsifal — for what they felt could not be put into words.

And then they all sat down in that great hall and made ready to see the wonder of the Grail. Once again, the spear was carried through the hall — and then came the maiden who carried the shining chalice whose light was nourishment.

When it was all over, black-and-white Feirefiz said: "I saw a beautiful maiden who held her arms as if she carried something — but there was nothing in her hands. Why did she act in this fashion?"

And then he was told that, being a heathen, he could not see the Grail. But Feirefiz wanted to see the Grail — and he also had lost his heart to the maiden, Repanse de Joie, who was the only one allowed to carry the Grail.

So Feirefiz, the black-and-white knight, was baptized and became a Christian, and he became the husband of her who carried the Grail. It was, after the king, the next highest honour amongst the servants of the Grail.

The next day, after Parsifal had become Grail King, Cundry, the messenger, brought the news that Sigune had passed away in the hut with her bridegroom's coffin — and, at Parsifal's order, Sigune and her bridegroom were buried in one grave.

Parsifal himself remained the King and Guardian of the Grail. Two sons were born to him and Condwiramur. They both became great knights, and the adventures of his elder son, Lohengrin — the knight of the white swan — form another one of the stories written by the troubadours.

And they say that this son of Parsifal became the last of the kings of the Grail. After Lohengrin, the son of Parsifal, the spear and the chalice were given to someone called "Prester John" — the Priest John — who guards it in secret, and can only be found by means that cannot be said openly.

The story of Parsifal — who set out as a fool and learned compassion through suffering — that story ends with his finding the Grail, and becoming its Guardian. Yet there is much that happened in the Parsifal story, to the whole story, in later centuries — in centuries after the troubadours. There even came a book, which is a kind of parody — a deliberate caricature of the Parsifal story and, as it happens, this parody is also one of the great works of literature. We shall first discuss some questions which arise from Wolfram's tale, and then go on to the parody that came later.

15

Feirefiz: Faith and Intellect

The last part of Wolfram's *Parsifal* raises a number of questions — such as, for instance, why he introduces at this stage this strange black and white man, Feirefiz.

But instead of simply telling you that he means — symbolically — this or that, I want you to discover the this meaning for yourselves. All I have to do is to provide you with the material first.

Now the first piece of material is a comparison — how the same thing appeared to the medieval mind, as compared to the modern mind.

A teacher of the Middle Ages would, for instance, say to his pupils: "A piece of charcoal is a dark, black lump. But once you get it burning, it gives light and warmth. The light and warmth are hidden in the coal — but once it is burning, the hidden light and warmth come out.

"And," the teacher would continue, "it is like this with you, my pupils. You have all kinds of faculties in you — you may not even know about them: they are still hidden. And my task as a teacher is to bring out that which is still a hidden faculty — to bring out the hidden flame that is waiting to be awakened." This kind of poetic picture was natural for the Middle Ages.

The modern mind does not speak like this about coal. The modern mind says: all plants contain a chemical called "chlorophyll." This chlorophyll has the peculiarity that it can absorb energy from the sunlight, and this energy is used by the plant. The plant takes carbon dioxide from the air, and breaks it up, by means of this sun energy, into carbon and oxygen. The carbon remains with the plant — the oxygen is returned to the air. The plant builds its body from the carbon. And when I burn wood or coal, I bring carbon and oxygen together again: the carbon is oxidized.

Now compare these two ways of looking at a piece of coal. The medieval man knew nothing of chlorophyll — or solar energy. He used the coal as a kind of poetic picture. But you can see that this poetic picture spoke to the feelings of his pupils. They did not learn any science from it — but it had a strong appeal to their feelings.

The modern scientific description does not touch any feelings, but it satisfies something else, something that is called our intellect. We would not be satisfied with a poetic picture — we want an intellectually satisfying explanation of what is going on in the world around us.

At the time of Wolfram, in the thirteenth century, there was precious little intellect amongst the people. It was, as I have told you, the Age of Faith, the age when the religious instinct provided people with all the explanations they needed. They did not need intellectual explanations — and if you had told them about chlorophyll or solar energy, they would not have understood it. The time for the intellect had not yet come.

Yet there was intellect already at that time — there was intellectual work on a great scale, but not in Europe, not amongst Christians. It was amongst the Muslims, amongst the Arabs.

In the seventh century, Muhammad had led the Bedouin tribes of Arabia out of the desert lands and commanded them to convert the unbelievers by fire and sword to the religion of Islam. Under their banner, the green flag with the crescent moon, the Arabs had defeated every army sent against them, until their conquests reached from Spain, over North Africa, to the Black Sea, and so formed, geographically, a half-moon or crescent around the south of Europe.

The Arabs they recognized a good thing when they saw it, and so they learned not only from the countries under their dominion, they learned from the great empires of the East, India and China. The Arabs had orderly minds and they were the first to bring all this knowledge from hundreds of sources together and to sort it out.

And so came the first universities, with divisions into various "faculties" or departments.

At a time when the whole of Europe possessed perhaps ten

thousand books, one Arab university in Cordoba alone had a hundred thousand books. At a time when in Europe only clergy of the higher ranks of the Church could read or write, the Arab universities had thousands of students learning physics, chemistry, astronomy, medicine.

And at a time when the Christian people of Europe had to work with an abacus, with beads on strings, if they wanted to work out a difficult sum like 15 x 12, the Arabs brought from India the so-called Arabic numerals, and worked out all the rules of arithmetic we have now. They took these rules even further, and started algebra — which is an Arabic word, meaning the "reunion of broken parts."

And if there is one thing which is purely intellectual, it is algebra. The Arab civilization, with its science, with its mathematics, was indeed a civilization of the intellect, and several centuries ahead of Christian Europe, which still lived in feelings and instincts — except for a few advanced minds here and there.

This was the position at the time when Wolfram wrote his *Parsifal*. But, as I have mentioned, the Albigenses, these Manichean heretics in Provence, were on the best of terms with their Arab neighbours across the Pyrenees in Spain. They knew and they admired the intellectual achievements of the Arabs.

And so did the secret Manichean, Wolfram. He speaks in one part of the story of the movements of the planets, and he calls them "Zval," "Almustri," "Almuret," which are the Arab names for Saturn [*Zuhal*], Jupiter [*Al Mushtori*], Mars [*Al Ahmar*]. Wolfram knew something of the scientific and intellectual civilization of the Arabs.

But Wolfram could see further than that. We know already that he could foresee a time when the instinctive religious feeling of his own time would die out, would disappear. But whilst this instinct grew less and less, something else would grow more and more — the intellect. Those two things go together — it is just like the phases of the moon. As the dark part grows smaller, the silvery crescent grows bigger. And as the instinctive religious feeling began to withdraw, there began in Europe the growth of intellect.

And Wolfram, the heretic — who knew both sides, who

loved the Christian faith but also admired the intellectual knowledge of the Moors — Wolfram could foresee a time when the growing intellect in Europe would reach out and welcome the intellectual knowledge of the Moors.

At the time of Wolfram, there were not many such people yet. There were some, however, and one of them was a Scotsman. He came from the border country around Abbotsford and Dryburgh Abbey. His name was Michael Scot. This Michael Scot went all the way to Cordoba in Spain and studied at the great Arab university there. But when, after many years of travel in Italy and Germany, he came back to his native Scotland, the people felt there was something uncanny about a man who had learned intellectual knowledge — it was something devilish. They feared him too much to burn him at the stake — but they did call him a sorcerer and a wizard, who had sold his soul to the devil.

And so, Michael Scot, the wizard, became a Scottish legend. But he was a real, historical person whose studies in Cordoba and Toledo made people in Scotland highly suspicious of him. Again here was someon willing to approach secret, "heretical" ideas with an open mind, and that made him seem dangerous.

In Wolfram's time, most people still felt that there was something uncanny and devilish in the cold light of the intellect of the Moors. They felt their own, instinctive religious feeling as a warmth, like the light of the sun, and the Arabs' intellectual knowledge as a light that gave no warmth, like the light of the moon. And they wanted no part of it.

And in Wolfram's time there were still Crusaders — Christians and Muslims fought each other grimly. The Crusaders still thought they could conquer the Muslims — and the Muslims still thought of conquering Europe one day.

Yet Wolfram, in his intuitive knowledge, foresaw a time when the warm, instinctive forces would come to an end, when Europe itself would be ready for the intellect, and would receive the intellectual knowledge of the Arabs with open arms.

And now, think of this situation: Crusaders and Moors fighting each other in the Orient, but Wolfram realizing that there would be no winners in this fight, and that, in future, something had to come from the Moors, something they had achieved before Europe: intellectual knowledge. And in this situation, you have the answer to the riddle of Feirefiz, the elder half-brother of Parsifal — Feirefiz, the king of the Moors.

Feirefiz is the intellect, the intellectual knowledge that the Moors had, that was born amongst the Moors, before it came to Europe. And Parsifal can only meet Feirefiz, the intellectual knowledge, when he has lost the religious instinct, when religion, as his time knew it, no longer meant anything to him.

He has lost the religious instinct, and from now on, that which came from the Moors was to be his companion and brother — we could say: a part of himself.

Parsifal, the hero of the future, cannot depend on religious feelings — he must find his way with intellect, as we all must do now: that is the meaning of the meeting with Feirefiz.

But why is Feirefiz black-and-white? Wolfram wanted to point out something very important about intellectual knowledge. For a Manichean, like Wolfram, darkness and light, black and white, were not just colours. For a Manichean, black stands for evil and white stands for good.

Now take a man who is intellectually very gifted: he has a brilliant intellect — does this make him also a good man? No — he can use his intellect for good or for evil, and a good many people use it sometimes for good and sometimes for evil. The intellect, for itself, is neither, or it is both good and evil — it has both possibilities, it is black and white.

Wolfram could see just that far. But we, today, know much more about the "black-and-whiteness" of the intellect than Wolfram ever did.

Take just some of the achievements of intellectual science. It has prolonged human life and reduced infant mortality. That's pure white. But it has, at the same time, created the problem of over-population. There is not enough food in the world to feed the hungry millions in India and China — and the situation will be worse in fifty years' time. Will they die of starvation — will they go to war to expand their living-space at the cost of others? It is in any case a black picture.

The intellect has created a wonderful vehicle for locomo-

tion, the motor car. But think of the congestion and the pollu-
tion to our planet.

It would not be difficult to make a long list of things created
by the intellect which are a blessing and a curse, good and evil,
black and white at the same time.

So, when Wolfram chose a black-and-white man as personi-
fication of the intellect, it was a very apt picture — apter than he
knew.

But, whether we like it or not, we cannot do without intellect — it has become our constant companion, as Feirefiz
became the companion of Parsifal. And, we are told in the story,
that when Parsifal is called to the Grail, he is told he must bring
the black-and-white man with him.

The search for the Grail is the search for God, for the divine
spirit in the world. In the past, it was feeling, it was instinct
which gave man the conviction that there is a God, that there is
a spiritual world besides the world of the senses.

This instinct works no longer, or only in a few people. Today,
if anyone seeks at all to find a new meaning in the old words, he
must seek with his intellect — he cannot leave his intellect
behind.

If there is any answer to the quest of the Grail, then this
answer must also satisfy the intellect, and not only in feelings and
emotions. One could say — for our time, a religious path to the
Grail is not enough, it must be an intellectual, a scientific path.

And that is why Parsifal, a hero of our time, can only come to
the Grail with his black-and-white companion.

But we are told that Feirefiz, when he comes to
Montsalvage, cannot see the Grail, until he is baptized and
becomes a Christian.

It is something that happens all the time — it happens specially amongst the most intellectual people of today, the scientists, that they stand before wonderful revelations of God's
wisdom in the world, and do not recognize them for what they
are.

But sometimes one of the great scientists does realize what
he beholds, and tries to convey what this experience is. Such a
great modern scientist was Einstein.

Einstein's "Theory of Relativity" is about the most abstract intellectual construction ever conceived by a human mind, and is as important for the modern astronomer as it is for the atomic scientist. Yet this great intellect, this great scientist, said the following words: "The most beautiful thing we can experience is the mysterious. It is the source of all true art and science. He to whom this experience is a stranger, who cannot pause to wonder and stand rapt in awe, is as good as dead. His eyes are closed."

Einstein says, in other words: There is something in the world for which I have no words — I call it the mysterious. I can experience it, and those who can't are as good as dead or blind.

Einstein is a kind of Feirefiz, an intellectual who has seen what the little scientists do not see.

The figure of Feirefiz is not the only puzzle in the Parsifal story — there is the question of what does Sigune mean, the woman with the dead bridegroom? Or what is the meaning of Cundry? or Amfortas?

But it is not necessary to get all the questions answered in a work of art like *Parsifal*. It is a good thing to have questions, and to live with them.

In the next chapter we shall go from Wolfram's *Parsifal* to a great work of literature which is a kind of parody of it.

Don Quixote

The story of Parsifal was written about 1200 — it was just one of many "romances" which glorified the "quests" of knights and praised the virtues of chivalry. The troubadours had started this kind of story and it became very popular. One hundred, two hundred, three hundred years later, stories of knightly adventures were still highly popular — but the authors who produced these stories were no longer "troubadours," they were no longer people who wished to convey some great meaning in the form of pictures. Some of those later writers, like Spencer, did not bother to make their heroes into living beings, human beings of flesh and blood. The knights in Spencer's *Faerie Queen* are personifications of this or that virtue, but you can never feel with them, or for them, as you can with Parsifal. They are not flesh and blood, but allegories.

Other writers took quite a different line. They realized that what made people read such a story was the thrill of danger, of adventures — and the flights of fantasy. And so they invented as their heroes knights who were incredibly handsome, incredibly virtuous, incredibly brave, heroes who never put a foot wrong (as Parsifal had done) — and these authors also invented maidens of incredible beauty, attacked or endangered or enslaved by monsters, demons, giants, dragons, wizards, and of course the brave knight unfailingly killed and destroyed the monster and rescued the beauty in distress.

The love scenes in these stories were sheer pretentious tripe, the battle scenes became ever more wildly exaggerated, and the villains of the piece — sorcerers, giants — ever more impossible creatures, without rhyme or reason. *But there was no longer any deeper meaning at all in these stories.*

Yet, these later romances still sold like hot cakes. Printing had already been invented, more people could read and write, and they bought the stuff — they wallowed in it, they lapped it up. This is all the more surprising, as by then the time of knights and of chivalry was already past. Gunpowder had been invented, and made armour quite useless. America had been discovered, science was in its beginning, the Reformation was shaking all traditional beliefs — so what use was a knight in armour in this new world?

But it seems as if the people were, in a way, scared of this new world that was dawning, as if they wanted to escape — at least in their reading, in books — to the past, to a time of brave knights, of wizards and magic. And so, at the very moment when the real knight became an antiquity, when chivalry and knighthood were finished for good, at that moment of history, people all over Europe read avidly stories about utterly unreal knights, and about utterly meaningless and wildly fantastic quests of one kind or another. People read these stories to escape from the real world in which they lived.

And so we come to the time around the year 1600. By that time, Spain already had large colonies in America, England had become Protestant, Spain had sent the great Armada against England, and the Armada had been destroyed.

Yet, at that time, four hundred years after Wolfram and his Parsifal, people were still reading these stories of handsome knights, noble maidens and fearsome monsters.

And then, about this year 1600, a Spaniard wrote a book which made an end of all this — it is a book that belongs to the great works of art, and it is also one of the few funny books in world literature.

The man who wrote the book, Miguel de Cervantes, was a soldier and adventurer (he lost his left hand in a sea battle with the Turks, and was for five years a slave in Turkish captivity). Cervantes knew from his own experience the real adventures of his own time, and he saw how ridiculous the fictitious, invented adventures of these romantic stories were. And so he wrote his book, *Don Quixote,** in which he exposed the foolishness of all the other stories so popular in his time.

---

* Pronounced *Don Kee-hoti,* or, particularly in Britain, *Don Quick-sot.*

This book, *Don Quixote,* is also the first real novel — that means a novel about real people, and the real world they live in. It is a long story — and I am very sorry that I can only give a little time to it, for it is a masterpiece.

The hero of the story is an elderly gentleman, Quesada by name, a gaunt, haggard man with hollow cheeks and a little pointed beard. This man, well over fifty, owns some land in a village in Spain and has a few farm-hands who work for him, and so he has plenty of time to read books. He loves to read books — but only one kind of book, the books about knights and quests and heroic adventures.

He reads and reads — and in time the fictitious heroes become more real to him than the world around him. His brain becomes completely befuddled by these wild and woolly stories — he comes to believe that all these knights he reads about are real persons, be believes that the wizards and dragons and giants exist really somewhere in the world.

And, in the end, he is so caught by this madness, that he decides to become himself such a glorious knight. His name, Quesada, an ordinary Spanish name, is not good enough for a knight going on a quest, so he calls himself "Don Quixote."

A knight must have a lady in whose honour he performs great deeds and to whom he sends all the enemies he has overcome in single combat. Our poor Don Quixote, a dried-up elderly bachelor, has no lady, but he sees a buxom village girl (she milks the cows next door) and he decides that she is to be the lady to whom he will send his captives and, as her name is also ordinary, she is re-christened in his mind "Donna Dulcinea."

But what about armour? Don Quixote finds in the attic rusty bits of armour from his great-grandfather's day and fits them together with bits of string and wire. He has some difficulty with the helmet, for the visor, the piece that covers the eyes, is missing, but he makes himself a visor from cardboard and ties it with strings on to the helmet. There is a spear, and an ancient rusty sword, and a badly dented shield — but to Don Quixote they are wonderful shining weapons, to defy all the monsters of the world.

And, finally, there is a miserable old carthorse in his stable, a creature with every bone sticking out — but to Don Quixote the horse is a beautiful mare, and is given the name "Rosinante."

There is a woman housekeeper and a young niece who look after him, but Don Quixote is well aware that these good, practical women have no understand for chivalry and for the great destiny that is in store for him. And so he does not tell them of his intentions, but one day, when they are both out, he gets into his rattling pieces of armour, mounts the noble horse, Rosinante, and armed with his priceless weapons, rides out on his quest.

The first adventures go — as can be expected — badly for him. People think he is mad — they laugh at him in his silly outfit, or play up to him for fun and regard it as a great joke.

Then Don Quixote meets some people driving mules on the road. He stops the mule drivers and demands of them that they should acknowledge to him that there is no more beautiful woman in the world than his lady "Donna Dulcinea." The mule drivers tell him not to be a nuisance and to make way, whereupon Don Quixote lowers his spear and spurs his horse. Poor Rosinante makes an effort to gallop, but stumbles over her own feet and falls down, throwing Don Quixote off a few yards away.

The armour is too heavy for him to get up, and the mule drivers, enraged by his aggressive manner, take their sticks and give him a thorough thrashing.

After this misadventure, Don Quixote limps home, to the ministrations of housekeeper and niece, but he is not cured. Soon he sets out again, but this time with a "squire," a simple, down-to-earth peasant, Sancho Panza, who is persuaded by the hope of great treasures which Don Quixote promises, when he has killed a few wizards.

And so we come to the most famous of Don Quixote's adventures.

Soon after their departure, the knight and his squire came in sight of thirty or forty windmills which rise from that plain, and as soon as Don Quixote saw them, he said, "Fortune is guiding our affairs better than we ourselves could have wished. Do you see over yonder, my friend Sancho Panza, thirty or more huge giants? I intend to do battle with them and slay them!"

"What giants?" said Sancho, amazed.

"Those giants you see over there," replied his master, "with long arms — some of them are almost two leagues in length."

"Take care, sir," said Sancho, "those are not giants, but windmills, and the things which seem to you their arms are their sails which, when they are whirled round by the wind, turn the millstones!"

"It is clear," answered Don Quixote, "that you are not experienced in adventures. Those are giants — and if you are afraid, turn aside and pray whilst I enter into fierce battle with them!"

Uttering these words, he clapped spurs to Rosinante, without heeding the cries of his squire, Sancho, who warned him that he was not going to attack giants, but windmills. But so convinced was he that they were giants that he neither heard his squire's shouts, nor did he notice what the things were, even when he came near them. Instead, he rushed on, shouting in a loud voice: "Flee not, you cowards — one knight alone attacks you!"

At that moment, a slight breeze arose, and the great sails began to move. When Don Quixote saw this, he shouted again: "Even though you flourish a thousand arms, you shall pay for your insolence!"

With these words, he covered himself with his shield, couched his spear, charged at Rosinante's full gallop and rammed the first mill that stood in his way.

He ran his spear into the sail, but the wind twisted it with such violence that it shivered the spear to pieces, dragging him and his horse after it, and rolling him over and over on the ground, sorely damaged.

Sancho Panza rushed up to his assistance as fast as his donkey could gallop, and when he reached the knight he found that the poor man was unable to move, such was the shock that Rosinante had given him in the fall.

"God help us!" said Sancho. "Did I not tell you, sir, to mind what you were doing — for these were only windmills! Nobody could have mistaken them unless he had windmills in his brains."

"Hold your peace, dear Sancho!" answered Don Quixote, "for in knights' quests things can change very strangely. I am convinced that a magician has changed those giants into windmills to deprive me of the glory of victory ... But in the end his evil arts will be of little avail against my good sword."

"God settle the issue in his own way!" cried Sancho, as he helped his

master to rise and to remount Rosinante, who was almost disjointed by
the fall.

The knight and his squire were still discussing the last adventure,
when they saw a large, dense cloud of dust rolling towards them. Don
Quixote turned to Sancho and said: "This is the day on which I shall
show the might of my arm, and on which I shall do deeds that shall be
written in the book of fame for ages to come. Do you see that dust cloud?
It is churned up by a mighty army marching this way."

"If so, there must be two armies," said Sancho, "for here on this side
there is as great a cloud of dust!"

Don Quixote turned round to look at it, and seeing it was so, he
rejoiced, for he fancied there were indeed two armies coming to fight each
other. In fact, the clouds of dust were raised by two large flocks of sheep,
rams and ewes, which were being driven along the same road from opposite directions but, owing to the dust, they could not be seen until they
came near.

Sounds could be heard, and Don Quixote said, "Can you hear the
neighing of horses, the blaring of trumpets and the rattle of the drums?"

"I hear nothing," answered Sancho, "but the bleating of sheep and
lambs."

"You are a coward!" said Don Quixote angrily, "and the fear you are
in allows you neither to see nor to hear correctly, for it is the effect of fear to
disturb the senses. But if you are so afraid, stand aside, and leave the
fighting to me, for I alone am sufficient to give victory to the army whose
side I am going to take!"

And with these words, he gave Rosinante the spurs and, with his
spear couched, rode down the hillside like a thunderbolt.

Sancho shouted to him, "Come back, master — I swear to God that
those you are going to charge are only sheep! There are no knights or
shields! What are you doing?"

Don Quixote, however, did not turn back, but charged on, shouting
at one of the dust clouds to follow him against the other one. And then he
dashed into the midst of the flock of sheep and speared some of them with
such fury, as if he were fighting his mortal enemies.

The shepherds who came with the flock shouted at him to leave off,
but seeing that words were of no avail, they began to throw stones at him
as big as a fist. Don Quixote took no notice of the stones, but galloped to
and fro, shouting that the king of the enemies should come forward and

fight him, man to man. But then one stone hit him in the ribs, a second hit his mouth and broke a few teeth, and a third one crushed two fingers of his hand. And when another stone fell with great force on his helmet, Don Quixote fell off his horse and on to the ground, and lay unconscious. The shepherds thought they had killed him, and they quickly collected the half dozen dead sheep and drove their flocks away in great haste, without further enquiry.

All this time, Sancho had stood on a hillock, watching his master's mad escapade, tearing his beard, moaning and cursing. But seeing him lying on the ground, and the shepherds out of sight, he came down the hill to help his master, who was just regaining consciousness.

He said: "Did I not tell you that those were not armies, but sheep?"

To which Don Quixote answered: "That accursed wizard has again used his black art and made the men change into sheep! But if you would follow them, you would see that, as soon as they are out of my reach, they become again an army on the march!"

It is not possible tell you all the hundreds of adventures of Don Quixote — how he took a country inn for an enchanted castle, or how he held a waterfall at bay all night, and so on. I will end up by relating how he acquired a magic helmet:

There were two villages, but only one of them had a barber, and this barber used to come two or three times a week to the other village to shave the men who did not want to grow beards. On these occasions, he took with him a basin in which he made the soap lather for his customers. He was on one of these journeys, riding on a mule, when a light drizzle began to fall; as the barber did not want his new hat to get stained by rain, he took it off and put the basin on his head, for he did not like to get his hair wet. To his misfortune, he encountered on the way Don Quixote and Sancho Panza.

Don Quixote took the barber to be a knight with a helmet of gold. And when he saw the poor fellow draw near, he shouted a challenge, and with lance couched, galloped at him.

The barber, seeing so unexpectedly this wild apparition dashing against him, had no other way of avoiding the thrust of the spear than to fall off his mule. But no sooner did he touch the earth, than he sprang up, more nimbly than a deer, and ran away, leaving the basin on the ground behind him.

Having driven his enemy to flight, Don Quixote was satisfied, and told Sancho to pick up the "helmet." Sancho lifted it and said:"That's a good basin — worth a couple of shillings anywhere!"

But Don Quixote took it from him and put it on his head — and was only surprised that the lower half, the visor, was missing. He said: "This enchanted helmet must have fallen into the hands of someone who did not know what a wonderful thing it was — and so he melted one half of the pure gold down, and changed the other half so that it may appear like a barber's basin. But I shall wear it just the same, for I know its true worth and magic!"

With this story, we leave the brave knight, Don Quixote, a man who really had some of the qualities of the true knights — courage, love for battle, the wish to combat evil — but, alas, lacked common sense and lived in a world of fantasy and illusion. And we also leave Sancho Panza, who had commonsense, but could not understand noble ideals and principles at all.

It is a long story — it tells not only the escapades of Don Quixote, but give at the same time a most realistic picture of life in Spain at that time. That it is why it is the first novel in the modern sense — a novel about real people, and the real world they live in.

In the end, Don Quixote returns to La Mancha, his home village, and falls ill. But as death approaches he awakes from his dream of knights, and he dies with a clear mind, whilst Sancho Panza cries and weeps at the loss of a master who — even in his folly — was a good man, a man who strove for goodness.

Sancho Panza's Common Sense

We are all familiar with a figure which is both funny and pathetic — the person who does not want to grow old, and who, in her forties or fifties still dresses and behaves like a girl of twenty. There is something pathetic and grotesque about an older person trying desperately to act the part of youth. There is a rather cruel but apt description for such a person — people say with a shrug: "Mutton dressed as lamb."

Such an unfortunate is Don Quixote. It is all right for the young Parsifal to be eager for glory, fame, the honours of knighthood, but the same bright eagerness in a man well in his fifties is plain silly.

Cervantes, the author of the Don Quixote story, makes his hero from the start a parody of Parsifal by giving him the same ambitions as Parsifal had — but as a man of fifty, when he should know better.

But Don Quixote does even worse than that. Humankind has grown older since the time of the troubadours — the age of chivalry is past — but Don Quixote hankers after that earlier, younger stage, and so tries to live in his own time as if knights and chivalry still existed.

Don Quixote is not only an elderly man acting like a young one, he is a man of the seventeenth century acting as if he lived in the twelfth century — he is an anachronism.

"Anachronism" means someone or something which does not fit into the time. Don Quixote, galloping about in his rusty armour in a time which already had cannons and muskets, is an obvious anachronism. There are other, less obvious anachronisms in the present time — they are just as ridiculous as Don Quixote on his noble steed, Rosinante.

So Don Quixote is an anachronism, a man who does not fit

into his own time. But neither did Parsifal: you remember I pointed out again and again that Parsifal, in spite of the medieval trappings, is a stranger in his own time, and so is Don Quixote.

What is the difference? Parsifal looks forward, into the future — he represents the future in his own time. Don Quixote looks backwards, he hankers for the past — he is a hero of the past.

You see, Don Quixote is in everything the opposite, the counterpart of Parsifal.

Parsifal is isolated from his time by his upbringing in the forest. For Parsifal the vast forest of Saltane is the wall which keeps him separated from the civilization of his time, and which makes him an "outsider."

What isolates Don Quixote, what makes him an outsider? Books, his library of romantic stories of knights. It is his reading, his books, which create a mental wall around him and make him an outsider, a stranger in his own time.

If you consider that the paper of the books is made from wood pulp, and comes from forest trees, so that Don Quixote's library is really a little forest, you see the subtle irony of Cervantes in making Don Quixote a victim of his books.

Parsifal is laughed at for his fool's dress, and his great ambition is to obtain a knight's armour. Once he has put on the red knight's armour, he is no longer an object of ridicule.

But Don Quixote is laughed at just because he wears a knight's armour — this armour is now something foolish, it has become a fool's dress.

Parsifal finds later on a companion in his quest, Feirefiz, who as we know stands for the intellect. Don Quixote also finds a partner — a squire, the stout little peasant, Sancho Panza.

Just as Don Quixote is a parody, a caricature of Parsifal, so Sancho Panza, the uneducated, crude peasant, is a caricature of Feirefiz.

But this companionship of Don Quixote and Sancho Panza became in the writing of Cervantes far more than a mere parody, it became in fact a story of modern man in his own right — it became a funny and exaggerated picture, but yet a true picture, of modern life.

There is Don Quixote, full of noble ideals, full of fine great ideas, but without any practical commonsense. He cannot recognize windmills for what they are, he cannot recognize sheep for what they are — and so all his lofty aspirations end in catastrophe, they end in complete failure.

And there is Sancho Panza, the sturdy peasant to whom ideas and ideals are as incomprehensible as Chinese. But he has one side of the thing called intellect — he is practical, he sees windmills and sheep for what they are. And every time his master embarks on one of his escapades, he tries to stop him, though in vain.

And so Don Quixote and Sancho Panza are a perfect picture of the idealist, the dreamer, and of the down-to-earth, practical person.

And these two characters are haunting the world right up to the present moment.

Take such a thing as the great organization of all countries of the earth, the United Nations, or UN.

It was founded as a great idea, a great ideal after the last war, with the intention to prevent any future wars. The nations of the world should settle any differences they had by discussion. And if two quarrelling nations could not come to an agreement, the whole assembly should decide by vote who was right or wrong.

A very beautiful idea, but there were already at the beginning Sancho Panzas who said it would not work. And they were right. Now, decades after the foundation, the UN is faced with the crisis of becoming an ineffectual bureaucratic talking-shop without teeth.

Yet, the Sancho Panzas were also wrong. In those fifty years, the UN has provided peace-keeping forces in several of the worlds trouble spots, as well as its work with health, education and care of refugees.

You see, if we listened only to the Sancho Panzas, no unselfish action, no moral deed would ever be performed — there would only be brutal self-interest ... and let the devil take the weakest.

But if we only listened to the Don Quixotes, we would be

forever dreaming up beautiful ideas for the benefit of all humankind — only these beautiful ideas would come tumbling down like a house built of cards as soon as they got in touch with reality.

And, in fact, there is a Don Quixote and a Sancho Panza in every one of us. Nearly everyone has some ideas on how the world could be put right — never mind whether the idea is practicable or not. And nearly everyone has that practical streak which says: look out for yourself, get as much as you can for yourself, and don't worry about the rest of the world. In some people the Sancho Panza is stronger, and in some people it is the Don Quixote.

You find the Don Quixotes and the Sancho Panzas in every walk of life. There is the painter who believes in his own genius, and will hunger and starve rather than paint something that could be sold easily. And there is the artist who works only for his bread and butter, and does not care in the least whether his products are great works of art or not.

There is the author who writes only books which contain, in his opinion, an important message, whether they have a big sale or not. And there is the "hack," as they are called, who will write anything that sells easily and quickly. You can find Don Quixotes and Sancho Panzas amongst doctors and lawyers, amongst Members of Parliament, and in government.

But there are also the people who are able to strike the right balance between them — people who are inspired by high ideas, but are also able to make them practical and workable.

I have already mentioned here Henry Dunant, the founder of the Red Cross. The idea which came to him after the battle of Solferino — the idea that all nations should agree to treat wounded enemies as they would treat their own — that idea was pure Don Quixote at the time, an impracticable fantasy. But he was also a practical man, a business man, and he made his idea a practical reality.

Or if Fleming had been only a Sancho Panza, he would have stopped going on with penicillin as soon as the "experts" condemned it. But he had enough of Don Quixote in him to carry on, even if he was called "fool." And in the end he succeeded.

Dr Barnardo was another one who had the right mixture of Don Quixote and Sancho Panza.

There is hardly anything great and good in the world that was not at first declared cranky, fantastic, the outcome of a deluded mind, and so these things might have been, if the people concerned had only been dreamers, Don Quixotes. But they could harness the plain commonsense of Sancho Panza to their dreams, and so make them real and practical.

And now you can see that Wolfram in his Parsifal story, and Cervantes in his story of Don Quixote, are both making the same point.

Parsifal cannot come to the Grail without the black and white Feirefiz, and Don Quixote must have his Sancho Panza beside him — or, in other words: high hopes and ambitions are fine, but you must have common sense trotting beside you.

But now, look at the whole thing from the side of Feirefiz, or from the side of Sancho Panza.

Would Feirefiz have come to the Grail without Parsifal? It is through Parsifal that Feirefiz is brought to the Grail. On his own, Feirefiz would never get to the Grail.

And what about Sancho Panza? Without Don Quixote, Sancho Panza would have remained all his life a brutish oaf, a coarse lout who could see no further than his next plate of sausage and onions.

But in all the silly escapades of his master, Sancho Panza comes to realize the noble motives, the high ideals, which move Don Quixote. And, although all those lofty ideals usually end with Don Quixote getting hurt, Sancho Panza learns to respect these ideals — he discovers that great ideals are something to be respected, even if they lead to dismal failure.

And so, when Don Quixote dies, Sancho Panza speaks with deep affection of his master, and with great respect. Don Quixote, a crank and a fool though he was, has lifted Sancho Panza from his oafish existence to an awareness of ideals, he has become a better man.

I said before that we each have something of Don Quixote in us, and something of Sancho Panza. And it is very tempting to think: I will let Sancho Panza have his way, I will follow Sancho

Panza and forget that silly dreamer, Don Quixote. But then Sancho Panza is the poorer for it — he will only become more and more brutish and oafish, and so will you.

And, you know, Cervantes, the writer who invented Don Quixote, who made such savage fun of this poor demented fellow who fights against windmills, Cervantes himself could not help liking Don Quixote — he could not help feeling a kind of kinship with Don Quixote. You can easily see why.

Take this famous battle with the windmills — Don Quixote sees something in the windmills which no-one else sees: giants, demons, monsters. But now, ask yourselves — what is a poet? A poet is a man who sees the same things you and I see, but he sees more, he seems something we do not perceive.

To be an artist, a poet or a painter, you must have a good dose of Don Quixote, a good dose of that imagination which could see monsters where we see only windmills.

I could well imagine a poet writing verses in which he compares a windmill — or, for that matter, any large piece of machinery — with a giant or a monster.

And if you think of some factory towns, darkened by smoke from belching chimneys, the idea of some smoke-belching dragon has come to more than one writer.

The poet needs some of that imagination which Don Quixote has. Of course, there is a difference between being carried away by his imagination, as Don Quixote was, and the poet who controls the imagination and creates a work of art.

But the vivid imagination must be there in the poet — and that is why the artist, the poet, the painter, will always have a weak spot for Don Quixote: he feels a distant kinship.

And the Sancho Panzas of the world, who only laugh at Don Quixote, are also the people to whom all art — poetry, painting, music — means nothing at all.

I said, once before, "... a good book not only tells a story — it tells you also something about yourself." Wolfram's *Parsifal* is such a "good book," and so is the story of Don Quixote.

Simplicissimus

The story of Don Quixote, a kind of parody of Parsifal, a Parsifal in reverse, was written round about 1600 — a short time after the Great Armada of Spain had been destroyed in the English Channel.

This story of Don Quixote marks the end of the "romances," the wonder tales about knights and fabulous quests. In 1600, the knight with his high ideals had been made ridiculous — a figure of fun — a creature who no longer fitted into the new ages.

And what now came over Europe were wars which were, indeed, no longer fought with any regard for the rules of chivalry. What now came over Europe were the Wars of Religion — the wars between Roman Catholics and Protestants. The worst of these religious wars was in Germany. It is called, after its long duration, the Thirty Years' War (1618–48).

The political details, the battles, the beginning and end of that Thirty Years' War, do not concern us here. It was a war full of inhuman brutalities, a war in which the soldiers of either party robbed, plundered and murdered the civilian population without much regard as to which side they were on.

Any troop of solders coming upon a village or homestead would regard the peasants as their legitimate prey, and do with them as they liked — burn houses and crops, and take the sheep and cattle.

At that time of terror, extending over thirty years, a German writer, Grimmelshausen, wrote a book that has also become one of the classics of world literature. It is the story of a little boy, suddenly orphaned by the horrors of this war. There are many parts of that story which even in our time, used to atrocities as we are, make hair-raising reading. But this boy, uneducated and ignorant, is also a kind of Parsifal, who enters the world without preparation. And he is a Parsifal who has very much come down in the world — he is not the son of a king and a fine lady, he is not even a landed gentleman, like Don Quixote, he is the son of simple peasants.

This boy is not going out into the world urged on by the desire for knightly honours, he is driven from his home when soldiers burn it down and kill his parents.

So, you see, with this book we are no longer in the world of lofty principles, of noble aims, of knights sworn to protect the weak and poor. We are in a world of harsh and brutal realities.

Yet, there is in this boy still something of the innocence, something of that purity, which was in Parsifal, which was in Caspar Hauser.

This boy — like Parsifal — does not know his name; the first person he meets eventually gives him a name: "Simplicissimus," which is Latin, meaning "the most simple-minded." And that is also the name of the book — *Simplicissimus.*

Now when you hear parts of this story, remember that there are children of this kind living today — orphans of wars they cannot understand, waifs and strays torn from their homes by some twist of politics; there are such children today in many parts of the world, in Cambodia, in Bosnia and in Rwanda in Africa. The tales of some of these children of our time might not be so different from the tale of this boy of the Thirty Years' War, three hundred years ago.

The story is told by the hero, Simplicissimus, himself, who remembers as a grown-up man the stormy events of his childhood.

When soldiers have burned the homestead, the boy runs away, not knowing where to go and what to do. He comes into a forest, and there he finds a hermit, and now the following dialogue takes place. Try and notice specially the similarities with Parsifal, but also the differences.

HERMIT: *What is your name?*
SIMPLICISSIMUS: *My name is "boy."*
H: *I can see well enough that you are not a girl. But how did your father and mother call you?*

S: *What is a father, or mother?*

H: *Well, who gave you that shirt you are wearing?*

S: *Oh, that was my mam.*

H: *And what did your mam call you?*

S: *She said: "boy" — or sometimes "rascal," or "silly ass," or "good-for-nothing."*

H: *Who was your mam's husband?*

S: *She had no such thing.*

H: *Surely there was a man living with her?*

S: *Yes, that was my dad.*

H: *What was his name?*

S: *His name was "dad."*

H: *Did your mam call him "dad," or did she sometimes use another name?*

S: *Yes — she called him sometimes "drunken pig," or "lazy brute."*

H: *You are an ignorant creature — you don't know your own name, nor the name of your mam and dad!*

S: *Neither do you, Mister Clever.*

H: *Have your mam and dad taught you to do God's bidding?*

S: *No, there was a girl who looked after our bedding.*

H: *Have you not been taught the Lord's Prayer?*

S: *That they did. Our Father which art heaven, hallowed name, to thy kingdom come, thy will come down on earth as it says in heaven, give us debts as we give our debtors, lead us not into temptation but deliver us from the kingdom, the power and the glory for ever. Amen.*

H: *God help us — do you know nothing about our Lord?*

S: *Oh yes — my mam brought him home from church and put him on the wall of the room we ate in.*

H: *You poor boy. If I only knew where your parents are, I would bring you home.*

S: *Wouldn't be much use — the house is burnt down.*

H: *Who were the people who burnt the house?*

S: *There were some iron men — they sat on things as big as oxen, but had no horns. And those men slaughtered our pigs and sheep and cows, and so I ran away, and then was the house burnt.*

H: *Where was your dad then?*

S: *Oh, the iron men took him and tied him up and put salt on the*

soles of his bare feet and then our old goat was set to lick his soles —
and dad laughed and laughed, and then in the end he told the iron
man where he had hidden a pot, and they dug it up and it was full
of round things that glittered.

H: *And what happened then?*

S: *I don't know. My mam had run away, and the girl screamed, and*
I ran away too, and the house was burnt. And now I don't know
where to go.

H: *You can stay with me, lad, and I will try to look after you, and to*
educate you as a good Christian.

The next part of the story is told by Simplicissimus himself —
he looks back, as a grown-up man — to his first weeks with the
Hermit:

Now when I first saw the Hermit read the Bible, I could not conceive
with whom he should speak so secretly, for I saw the moving of his lips,
yet no man spoke to him. I marked, however, by his eyes that it all had
something to do with the book.

So I marked where he kept it, and when he had laid it aside, I crept
there and opened it, and at my first attempt came upon the story of Job
and the picture that stood at the beginning of the chapter. I looked at the
figures in the picture, and I asked them all kinds of questions. They gave
me no answer, and I got very cross with them. "You little clowns!" I said.
"I know you talk well enough with the old man — so why do you pre-
tend to be silent with me? And I see you are up to no good, for that poor
chap's house is in flames, and no-one is doing anything about it. But you
wait — I'll get some water and quench the fire." I got up to fetch water,
when the hermit came in and asked: "Where are you going?"

"Look," I said, "I know what's going on in that book. The house is
a-burning, and soon there will be more iron men coming to kill the sheep
as they have done with ours!"

"Stay," said the Hermit, "can't you see these figures are not alive?" To
which I answered, "It's you who can't see what they are up to — but I
know, I have seen it all happen before. Keep an eye on the sheep whilst I
go to fetch water."

"Child," said the Hermit, "they are not alive — they are only made
to call up before your eyes things long past."

"How could that be?" said I, "seeing that you have long talks with them?" And then the Hermit could not help laughing, and said, "They can't talk — but what they do, and what they are, I can see from these black lines." But I answered, "My eyes are better than yours, and I can't see anything on the lines but black squiggles. So how can you see more than I do?" And he said, "I will teach you this art called 'reading,' and then you will see what I see in the lines."

The boy was — for his simple-mindedness — called "Simplicissimus" by the Hermit. He spent two years in the solitude of the forest with the old man, learned to read the Bible, and about the Christian faith, but nothing else about the world.

And then, after two years, the Hermit died, and Simplicissimus left the forest. He was a very strange-looking creature then, dressed in rags, with his hair growing down to his shoulders. He had some horrifying adventures, running into soldiers torturing peasants, and into peasants taking their revenge on the soldiers. But, in the end, he found the governor of a city who took pity on the waif who could not say where he came from, and did not know where he was going to. This governor had the boy cleaned up and employed him as a page.

But Simplicissimus was utterly ignorant of the ways of the world — he made terrible blunders, and the other servants in the household made things worse by playing on his foolishness. Such an occasion was when he saw a dance for the first time in his life. He tells again the story in his own words:

I saw in that room gentlemen and ladies twisting about so quickly that everything spun about, and with such stamping and noise that I deemed they had all gone mad. I could not imagine what they could intend with this rage and fury. The very sight was so terrible that my hair stood on end.

I saw that they were my governor's guests who, up till noon, had been in their right senses, and I wondered what had suddenly driven them to such madness.

I wanted to know what this insane behaviour could mean, and so I asked another servant in the room what all this lunacy was about. And he, with a very serious face, told me that all the people present had agreed to stamp down the floor of the room — they wanted to break the floor.

"Good heavens!" I said. "We are one floor up, and if the floor breaks, we shall all fall a long way, and break our legs and necks!"

"Yes, indeed," said the fellow, "but they have been drinking, and in their intoxication just don't care what's going to happen! What's more," he said, "when they feel that they are in danger of falling down, each man grabs a lady, for it is said that when couples fall, holding one another, neither partner will suffer any great harm."

I believed all this tale, and there fell upon me such a fear of cracking my skull or breaking my bones when the floor gave way that I knew not where to stand. And, just then, the musicians who had paused for a while struck up again, and I saw every man run to a lady, like soldiers when the trumpets sound the alarm. I expected that any moment now the floor would fall to pieces under me — I felt myself already plunging down. And now these madmen began to jump, so that I could really feel the floor shaking. I thought, "Now your life is at stake!" and in my deadly fear I looked for a partner to fall down with.

I saw a very noble lady in a corner, in conversation with my governor. I caught her all unawares by the arm, like a bear, and clung to her — but then she struggled to shake me off. I was in real despair, and started to scream as if they would murder me.

The music stopped all of a sudden — the dancers and their partners stopped their hopping, and the noble lady complained loudly about that lout (meaning me) who still clung desperately to her arm.

My governor was greatly annoyed, and commanded I should be soundly whipped and then locked up somewhere. Yet the grooms who had sympathy for me spared me the whipping and locked me up in a goose-pen under the staircase.

Yet this same Simplicissimus who acts so foolishly looks with his childish mind upon the world in which he finds himself, and observes things which the normal "clever" people never notice. He says:

When I was with my old Hermit, I had always wondered why God had made it a law that one should not worship idols. Why should anybody be so silly as to worship anything else but God? But no sooner had I come into the great world, than I marked how wellnigh everybody had his own special idol to worship. Some had their god in their moneybags, and they put all their trust in this god. Others made popularity their god, and they fancied that this god would lift them up to become half gods themselves. And there were women, who made their own beauty their idol. Every day, instead of other offerings, they adorned that god with paint, ointment, powders, and gave many hours to the service of that idol.

Even as much of these, and a great number of other idols, were worshipped, so the true God was held in contempt. I had read of Christ's command that we should not only love our brothers, but even our enemies. Yet, amongst those who called themselves Christians, there was not only hatred of enemies, but so much envy and malice and quarrels between brothers, and brothers and sisters, and parents and children, as if they had never heard of that command.

As to the competition between businesses of the same trade — I would not have thought it possible that a man should wish another man's ruin in order to increase his own profits!

And I wondered still more when I saw people sit down in a game of cards or dice. Of them that took part, only one could win, but they all expected to win, which was utterly foolish — yet they who did so called me a simpleton.

It came to me that be honest and God-fearing and considerate of others was to be stupid in this world — but I would rather be that kind of fool than be called clever and be of their kind!

This Simplicissimus, this late Parsifal, of three hundred years ago, is — as you see — much nearer to our time, and a good deal that this simple-minded fellow said could just as well be said in the present day.

The Pure Fool

Parsifal, Don Quixote and Simplicissimus — the poor waif —
have all three something in common. And this 'common
denominator' is already present in the name of Parsifal.

I do not have to tell you that many books have been written
about Parsifal, and all these books try in one way or another to
interpret Parsifal's name. It is quite clear to every student of the
story that, as in Wolfram's story everything has a meaning, there
must be a special meaning in the name of his hero. But what this
meaning is — that is a point where opinions differ widely.

As the name is first used by Chrétien de Troyes, the French
troubadour, it is quite reasonable to assume that the name is
made up of French — medieval French — words. And then,
according to the old tongue, *langue d'oc,* as it is called, the name
would mean "through the valley" — that means a hero who
passes through the valley to gain the mountain peak, or in other
words, "through darkness into light." That is one interpretation.

However, in that ancient French language, the Langue d'Oc,
there were no uniform spelling rules, and with a slightly different spelling the name could mean "pierce the veil" — it means
a hero who sees his life and his destiny first veiled — he does
not know what he is meant to do, but in the end he breaks
through the veils, the veils are pierced. That is a second interpretation.

There is still a third one. The German musician, Wagner,
was not a professional etymologist — the science which deals
with the origin of words is called "etymology." His profession
was to write operas — and he is in the world of opera what
Beethoven is in the world of symphonies.

Now Wagner wanted to write an opera, *Parsifal* — in fact, he
did write it, and I only wish you could go to hear it: it is often

performed at Easter, for some of the most moving music ever written is contained in the scene where Parsifal meets the Hermit on Good Friday.

Now when Wagner was working on this opera, *Parsifal,* he did not go about it as any other composer would — Verdi, or Mozart, for instance. If they had a story they liked, a plot they liked, they were only concerned to get the music for the story — they were not worried about the origin of the story.

But Wagner, being a German, had this Teutonic streak of thoroughness — he had to go into every detail: where the story came from, what did Wolfram mean, what is the meaning of the name "Parsifal"?

And he came up with a different answer. His idea was to ask: what does "Parsifal" mean in the Persian language? It had not occurred to anybody else — but when you consider that both Chrétien de Troyes and Wolfram were adherents of that Manichean heresy which originated in Persia, it is not as far-fetched as it may sound. It would be quite in keeping with their ideas — and, moreover, the Persian meaning of the word "Parsifal" does convey something important and significant about the character of the hero.

In Persian, "Parsi-fal" means "the pure fool."

And, as you remember, both Chrétien and Wolfram go to great lengths to describe Parsifal in the beginning of the story as a "pure fool." Parsifal is very foolish when he asks the knights in the forest such questions as whether they were born with the armour on them — he is very foolish when he rides his horse into King Arthur's banqueting hall. But there is at the same time a childlike innocence, a childlike purity above the foolishness.

You only have to think of the story of Caspar Hauser, and you find in Caspar Hauser the same ignorance, the same foolishness, but at the same time this freshness, innocence, which is meant by the word "purity."

But I can give you an example of this "purity and foolishness" much nearer to us. Go to the kindergarten and look at some of the paintings done by little children. These kindergarten paintings are crude, primitive, foolish things: no house looks like a real house, and often one is not certain what it is the children painted. Yet, in these childish and foolish things, there is that innocence, that purity which makes these things something one can enjoy, something one can love, in spite of its being primitive.

And that kind of innocence and purity is also in Parsifal, the pure fool.

But now what about Don Quixote? He is not young, he is dried-up and elderly — he is a fool who tilts at windmills — but his foolishness, too, has something childlike.

The children in the kindergarten take a bench and call it a boat, they crawl under a table and call it a cave or a house — and I remember from my own childhood that I used to knock down large thistles and nettles with a stick, pretending they were giants. Children live in a world of make-believe, in a world of imagination.

And Don Quixote, too, like a child creates a make-believe world around him, but there is no cunning in him, he has no clever tricks to take advantage of others — and is, at heart, as simple as a child.

Don Quixote, too, is a "pure fool," a fool who has retained a childlike purity.

And our last hero, Simplicissimus, is a real child — he is still a young boy when the horrors of war destroy his home and family. And he tells the Hermit of these horrors with that candid innocence of a child that does not yet understand cruelty. He retains this innocence when he leaves the forest. Like Parsifal, he has been isolated by the forest, and so enters the world in ignorance and makes foolish mistakes — he becomes the butt of jokes by people who feel themselves wonderfully clever if they can make a trap for the ignorant boy.

But then the simpleton looks at the world around him, and his fresh and candid outlook is a good deal saner than the corrupt mentality of the people around him.

Simplicissimus, too, is a "pure fool."

But now I want to tell you about another such "pure fool," a fool who does not belong to literature, but to another medium of entertainment, to film — Charlie Chaplin.

Chaplin, too, presented in his films a little fool of a man, a down-and-out tramp, in grotesquely ill-fitting clothes, ignorant and not at all clever in the ways of the world.

In one of his films, *Modern Times,* he is employed in a great factory, and the little man goes through hair-raising and wildly funny misadventures in his encounter with machines and with the assembly line. But, you know, when you see that film your feeling, your sympathy is always with him, with that ridiculous little man — you laugh with him, and not at him. That is how you laugh when a child says something that seems silly.

Charlie Chaplin was also one of the "pure fools" — like Don Quixote, Simplicissimus and Parsifal.

I think you can feel now that there is something special about these "pure fools" who turn up here and there as heroes in literature or on the screen. There is something special about them — and I want to conclude this main lesson by telling you what it is that these childlike and silly people have.

Some years ago a well-known writer, Arthur Koestler, wrote a book called *The Act of Creation* — it is a very thick volume which tackles a problem that no-one has tackled before.

The problem is this: there are certain people whom we call "creative." Some are scientists, some are doctors, some are poets, painters, musicians — but they have one thing in common: they are able to create something new, something which is not a repetition, a copy, an imitation, but new and original.

But although each one of them at times had great difficulties in getting his discovery or invention or creation recognized, in the end what they had to give succeeded — it had to succeed because the world and all the millions who cannot create depend on the few who have this gift. Civilization, progress, would come to a standstill without them.

It is therefore a question well worth asking: what happens when such a genius produces or invents or discovers something new?

And the author of this book, Koestler, took the trouble to collect as many facts as he could about the conditions under which one of these great men did find or discover something new.

And the first thing he discovered was that in this respect

there is no difference between the scientist or the inventor or the artist — the act of creation is the same, whether it is merely inventing a new gadget, or producing a symphony, or discovering one of the secrets of nature. In other words — what kind of idea I get depends not on my training, but how I get a new idea is the same, no matter what my education and training is.

And this "how" is always a kind of "going back," a kind of going back to a more primitive or childlike frame of mind.

First of all, such a man can look at a thing he has known for years, as if he saw it for the first time, as if it were something new, fresh — something never seen before.

As long as you feel "familiar" with something — you say, "Oh, I have seen it, I know it ..." you will not get a new idea about it at all. The first thing is to look at it as if you were a child, seeing it for the first time.

And the second thing is to be deeply and wholeheartedly interested in this "new thing," just as a child would be interested in a new toy. Without real concern, real interest, nothing grows.

And the third thing is to get into a waking "dreaming" about this thing, as a child would day-dream and invent all kinds of imaginary things about something he has seen or heard.

One great scientist, F.A. Kekulé (1829–96), the discoverer of the benzene formula on which 90% of all industrial chemistry depends, this great man discovered that formula in a kind of day-dream as he sat on top of a London bus. And he used to say to his students, "Gentlemen, the first thing you have to learn is to dream."

And it is the same with hundreds of other important and successful people — they used a dreamlike imagination, and let it roam about the thing that interested them, and after a longer or shorter time, the great idea came: first as a "hunch" and then as a certainty.

A fresh outlook, a lively genuine interest, and free play of imagination — that is the recipe. But these are the three things which young children have naturally — to them the whole world is new, and all new things interest them, and they do imagine all kinds of things easily. The creative person has to become childlike again, or he cannot be creative.

As this writer, Koestler, put it: you have to go back (back to childhood) to go forward with a new idea. It is like trying to make a great leap, a great jump — say, over a little stream. You go a few steps backward, to have space for a run — then up you run, and leap across the stream. And that is what every creative person has ever done — gone back to a moment of childish wonder, childish imagination, and from this moment of childishness he or she made the great leap forward that brought him or her to a new idea, success and fame.

In all creative people, there is something that remained childlike, something that remained — to use our words — a "pure fool." And it is this child in them, this pure fool, that made them creative.

And, you know, this rather new idea, that book by Koestler, is not quite so new as it seems.

In Grimm's fairy tales, there is the following story. Once upon a time, there was a king who had three sons — the two older sons were clever, but the youngest boy was very foolish: his mind was like that of a child. Now the king did not know to which one of his three sons he should leave the kingdom when he died. He decided he would give the three sons an almost impossible task, and the one who could perform the task should inherit the kingdom. The task the king gave to his three sons was this: they should bring him ten yards of linen, spun so finely that it could be put into one nutshell.

The first son went to Holland, for Holland was famous for its fine linen, but he could not find any linen fine enough to get ten yards into a nutshell. The second son went to Silesia, another country with a great reputation for fine linen, but he too had no success. The third one — the silly, childish youngest one — just walked about, got into a forest, and suddenly something fell right in front of him and split open. It was a nutshell with yards and yards of the finest linen in it! And so he inherited the kingdom.

This old fairy tale, which superficially seems rather pointless, makes in fact the same point as the modern author, Koestler. The childlike son, the pure fool can see a great and complicated problem in one comprehensive view — as we say, "in a nutshell" — and that is why he inherits the kingdom, quite rightly, just as all creative men to this day inherit the great kingdom of original thought, of new invention which brings the world forward

But, you see, all human creativeness, whether it is art or science or invention, has its source and origin in the one Being who is called the Creator. Every little human act of creation is like a tiny drop from that great ocean of creativeness that is called "God."

And in every tiny act of creation, even when it is only a new and original idea in an essay you write, in the smallest act of human creation you take part — you participate — in the all-creativeness which is the true nature of God.

It matters very little that Parsifal has turned against God — the conventional idea of God — but he has remained in his heart a pure fool, he has remained creative.

And that is why he can find the Grail, see the Grail and become King of the Grail — because, in the end, the creative power in himself can recognize and behold the true nature of God: creativeness.

Only he who can create can find the Grail, the true and unconventional meaning of God — God, the Creator.

The others — the people who only conform, who repeat what others have done, who never create anything — can only talk about God, they can call him Creator, but these are empty words. Only the creative spirit in man can truly and really understand the creative spirit in God.

That is why we say in the morning verse: "God's spirit lives and moves in light of sun and soul — in heights of worlds without, in depths of soul within."* The spirit that created the world lives as creative power also in soul — a drop from that great ocean of creative power that made the world.

But, to find this creative power in yourself, that tiny drop of the creative world power, you have to become a pure fool, like Parsifal — you have to become like a young child. And that is what is meant by the words in the Gospel, the words Christ

---

* Verse given by Rudolf Steiner for Waldorf Schools.

spoke: "Unless you become like little children you cannot enter the Kingdom of Heaven" (Luke 18:17).

But the Kingdom of Heaven is not a place — Christ himself said: "The Kingdom of Heaven is within you" (Luke 17:21); it is the kingdom of creative thought, of creative action. This is the kingdom which the foolish son in the fairy story inherits. The Kingdom of Heaven is the power, the ability to create — and that is also the kingship given to Parsifal.

But, after all, we have to grow up, we cannot remain little children — we have to become adults and live in an adult world, with the worries and problems and responsibilities of adults. And so we have to be adults and yet carry with us something of the child — otherwise we cannot be creative.

And this truth — to be adult and yet to carry the creative child with us — this task has also been put into a symbolic picture, a picture you are all very familiar with, but which you will perhaps now understand with a new meaning: the picture of St Christopher.

That picture of the strong man who carries the creative child on his shoulders, that picture is the symbol of what it means to be creative — to be adult, but to carry in one's soul the power of the child — to be adult, and yet to be able at times to become like a child, a pure fool: that is the meaning of St Christopher.

And that is also the meaning of the story of Parsifal, the pure fool who became King of the Grail.

Further reading

Sources

Death of King Arthur, The [*La Mort le Roi Artu*], Tr. by J. Cable, Penguin Classics.

Eschenbach, Wolfram von, *Parzival,* Tr. by A.T. Hatto, Penguin Classics.

—, —, Tr. by H.M. Mustard & C.E Passage, Vintage Books.

Malory, Sir Thomas, *Le morte d'Arthur,* 2 vols. Penguin Classics.

Matthews, John. 1996. *Sources of the Grail.* Edinburgh: Floris.

Sir Gawain and the Green Knight, Penguin Classics.

Troyes, Chrétiens de, *Perceval,* Penguin Classics.

Other books

Golden Blade, The. No. 33

—. No. 47. *The Quest for the Grail.*

Hutchins, Eileen. *Parsifal – an Introduction.*

Jung, Fran von. *The Grail Legend,*

Markale, Jean. *The Grail: The Celtic Origins of the Sacred Icon.*

Moffat, Alistair. *Arthur and the Lost Kingdoms.*

Phillips, Graham, *The Search of the Grail.*

Seddon, Richard. *The Mystery of Arthur at Tintagel.*

Stein, W.J. *The Death of Merlin.*

—. *The Ninth Century in the Light of the Holy Grail.*

Steiner, Rudolf. *The Holy Grail.*

Sussman, Linda. *The Speech of the Grail.*

Wyatt, Isabel and Margaret Bennell. *From Round Table to Grail Castle.*